Yoga

&

The Art of

Self Healing

 Guide

Channeled and written by
life coach shaman mother Sandra Van Olmen

Copyright © by Sandra Van Olmen, 2017

YOGA and the ART of SELF HEALING

Spiritual growth, inner Mastery awakening.

Another important book of the author is her Autobiography:
OUR JOURNEY INTO MASTERY

Contact for private readings or yoga retreats at Mallorca:
sandra8wellness@gmail.com
General website: www.sandravanolmen.com

ISBN-13: 978-1542574174

Grateful

I dedicate this book…
To each person who has the courage to live in personal integrity.

To those who wish to help and guide others,
mothers and fathers
yoga teachers,
school and sport teachers,
life coaches,
managers

To my students who taught me the art
of being a yoga apprentice in life itself.

Never forget dear leader…Just like the seagulls or pelicans who
fly in V-formation, also we, one by one take the lead.
I want to thank you for your trust, for letting me fly one moment
up front and cover you from the wind.
With this book I offer you the opportunity to feel empowered
when you take your turn up front. Guide your flock well.
Together we fly further, cover larger areas.

Namaste

Index

Resources for full potential

- Chakra awareness
- The brainwaves
- Reaching out to our loved ones from a distance
- The aliveness line
- The pendulum
- Nervous system. Saliva in our mouth = peaceful feeling
- The steps to activate fully the 7 chakras
- 7 powerful prayers/affirmations to work with the 7 chakras

Mastery

- Yoga, Vinyasa meditative info
- How to meditate, step by step
- Powerful wholeness healing and stem cell regeneration meditation
- How to OBE —out of body— astral travel
- Be successful
- Soul and Spirit
- Our personal gifted chakra
- Emma, her last wish granted
- Mexica Calendar: The Cosmic Tree

This book offers you all most of the tools that I use personally and teach in my **yoga retreats at the island of Mallorca**.

Restore 4 days/3 nights, enjoying yoga on the beaches, guided meditations, the mastery course, chakra readings, , shamanic cleansing ritual, paddle boarding, bo-staff practice and biking along the waterfront.

All year around, starting on Mondays and Thursdays

Feel free to write me for more info at sandra8wellness@gmail.com

The brain needs to understand in order for the heart to open up and allow the divine energy to activate itself.

When a person disbelieves, the magic fades!

With each new teaching…..

    First we feel curiosity about a certain subject

    we choose to know more about it

    after a while our mind starts to trust

    then our heart comprehends, we feel safe

    through practice

    we can accept and apply the teaching as "ours"

    our "truth"

    And as we have seen over and over…

    the *Truth* will set us *Free*

Part 1

Chakra- awareness

A re**sourc**eful powerhouse

We need to be aware of how powerful and influential our chakra system actually is.
The spiritual universe is made of colorful lights and void space, a highly intelligent, infinitely loving realm.
Towards the earth plane 7 specific colors with functional and purposeful attributes shine brightly and abundantly directly upon our body.

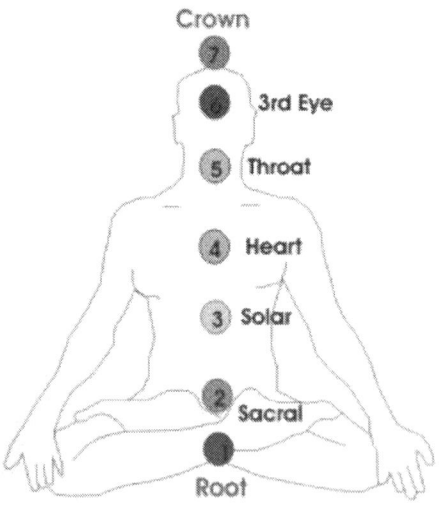

Our 7—invisible to the human eye—chakras located in our physical body are the link between the spiritual and the physical body. Our stem cell regenerating and restoring system uses the 7 physical glands, and the central nervous system to connect trough the chakras to the source and in each area the universal light is absorbed and transformed to energy that we can work with.

In order to live in pure harmony with our full potential, we need to keep our seven chakras activated in their full capacity of light, and as humans we, first and foremost, need to be as consciously aware of how we act/react in each moment of our daily life. Getting to know ourselves, only then can we apply "live and let live".

Many people have pets, but we don't set our pet free on the street before we trust that it comes back to us, or doesn't get itself in trouble. Once we "know ourselves" we can start building a "foundation" where we can live a grounded daily life within our full potential power. Meaning: fulfilled, peaceful, in enthusiasm, successful, warm hearted, powerful and not to forget healthy.

There is no separation between each chakra, yet each chakra has a different power and means to work with it in our daily life. This is the general information on each chakra, later on in the book we work deep upon each one.

First chakra - root

- Related to our lower physical body from the waist down, including legs, knees, feet. Located close to our genitals.
- Taking firm steps in pure intent.
- Be certain that you "belong", that your presence, actions, spoken words has meaning.
- Living with passion for life.
- Vitality activated:
  The power of kundalini, "the vital force of prana" existing in the air, when recognized, is consciously settled in the lower area of our body, then distributed in our entire body. One part of the vital force is passed to our stem cell system where it is used for us to remain within our physical potential, another part of the energy is used for mental activity, as in intellectual or creative, intelligence solution processes lowers a little more and then rises spiral wise up, around the spine towards the higher glands in our brain. If we can raise the energy to the upper glands, we can uphold a higher vision on life, but that is information is given when we work with the higher chakras.

Second chakra

- Live your daily life, grounded. Know and accept yourself.
- See your values, virtues and self-worth as important.
- Believe there is abundance in anything you truly need.
- Comprehend your emotions. Emotional balance is a big part of mastery and is extremely difficult since we are not living in a Buddhist monastery, we confront daily life as mothers, fathers, daughters, sons, employees. We are in the realm of influence from others.

  So the only solution we have is to comprehend how "drama" works, what triggers it and how to step away from it. If we are one of those people who have a habit established to become overwhelmed by emotional reactions, we need to use "maturity" and know this is one of our biggest rocks on our path. If the chemical anger, frustration or disappointment button triggers itself in you, don't linger in it. Don't dive fully in it, for we know we can't fully trust ourselves when we're in it and we know where it leads us. Breathe and be stronger and more mature that that basic impulse. Don't speak words you don't really feel from your heart, in' that passing by' situation in your life.
- Stop being dependent how others react or treat you. So confident you become dependent only on God, the intuitive inner knowing. Establish believes of your own, knowing where you stand pull it up from the first chakra, count on your roots. If you have pure intent, don't be afraid of the outcome. —Sometimes it happens that we make a mistake and find a treasure.

Third chakra

- Being creative beyond the known. Open up to intuitive action- and decision taking. Encounters with people that enhance your ideal of life. Reach into the Akasic Records and remember….Passed lives are no longer past; past life energy that you can tap into. The things you need, lifetimes you have earned your stripes. The power of Intuitive thought is a map through which you can take decisions to take, see your potential clearly.
- Become enthusiastic again, accept surprises, say "thank you" instead of "no thank you".
- Say "yes" and smile to the potential of the moment.
- Can you be lighthearted? The ultimate goal is to find the balance between being successful, mature yet like a child, open, enthusiastic and passionate. There face radiates with the love inside. Look past the face in the mirror, and see God reflected in your eyes.
- Accept prosperity, and think, decide and work towards it. Don't limit your thinking.

Fourth chakra

- The thymus gland is unlimitedly in love and will constantly remind us that we are made of that substance.
- Patience and tolerance is key in order to live in society and not go mad.
- Being able to live without creating drama, or to make things bigger than they are is to live free.
- Comprehension of other's needs.
- Open your heart, more compassion, more connection to others. Emphatic behavior is the greatest treasure we can live, it has a direct influence on our daily life, and offers prosperity if we can channel this to our professional expression.
- To be able to be humble and enjoy basic life, resonates in the center of your heart.

Fifth chakra

Three connections exist in this powerful blue chakra. The sky has many shades of blue, right?
1. Expression
2. Detachment
3. Inner communication

- Expression has an energy field around it. If it directed towards somebody, we need to be aware that "that field" provokes a chemical reaction in the other person. The more we are aware of it, the sooner we can take charge of it. Feel satisfied, content, become fulfilled. Feel the satisfaction in little victories.
And the way we express ourselves establishes who we are, and who we love to be. Spoken or thought affirmations!
- Detachment is a choice. How long do we wish to linger in something we know doesn't serve us. Resentment and disappointment dig themselves deep into our liver and kidneys and can cause lots of damage. At the first thought about something negative —as repetition or pattern established—, you can't get too deep, for you know it will hurt. Take charge. The back of your neck may start causing you pain and since this chakra is linked up to the second chakra directly, your lower back my suffer the consequences as well. And neck or -back pain is a killer!
- Inner communication. Give thanks to a perfect system. Digestion for one is important to be grateful for. You eat, before putting the first spoon in your mouth you close your eyes one moment and could say "Thank you for a perfect digestion of food, words and emotions. Please take care of those who have less." When you go to the bath room, comprehend how your body is perfect, and give thanks. In moments where you'll really need interdimensional communication with your stem cells —when sickness hits you— it will be tough if you haven't first established a habit. It's like a program you're not comfortable or certain with the procedure, you can't resonate at the height that is needed, hence people think they can't heal themselves.

Sixth chakra

- Meditate from one minute to one hour daily.
Enter the divine realm, —the theta brain wave state—, even if it is only a very short moment once or a few times a day.
Neo asked Morpheus "Why do my eyes hurt?" answer: "Because you've never used them before". Each time we enter in the divine realm, we experience one moment of pressure, as if our both eyes join in the center and become one. Then relaxation, a profound embrace touches us, warmly.
- Use the power of observation, look, yet don't participate emotionally in all your eyes see. Becoming a mere witness prevents us from "chemically exploding" inside.
- Non-judgmental behavior. No opinion. Watch and detach.
- When you look into the mirror, see your soul reflected in your eyes.

Seventh chakra

"Channel" your soul through your actions, words and thoughts. And do it in such a way that you yourself can actually feel the connection, from the lightness of your soul to the gratefulness of the person you're communicating with. The soul and spirit have the attributes of a wise child.

When this happens consciously, yin-yang energy in our body is restored in perfect balance. You hold your abundant share of the seeds of God in you, you can plant them for others and for yourself, anytime.

Live all the certainties you have established as "safe and beneficial", unlimited, they are in abundance.

Purifying

Before we can start making changes within our system, rather it is healing a certain pain or sickness, opening chakras or letting go of emotional disturbance, we first need to know the different means to cleanse our aura.
Our aura is the subtle exhibition of all the aspects of who we are, the manifestation of our physical and mental body, karmic structure, past and present are imprinted upon it.
What you manifested years ago may still obstruct your new possibilities. Old traumas may still hanging around you, not allowing you to become who you really want to be, or clouding you so you don't really feel as free or successful as your potential indicates.

Our body is a manifestation of several layers, some more profound than others, depending on how heavy we have taken it in our thoughts of emotional reactions.
The different layers need different approaches:
Food intake, meditation, chakra balancing, yoga,.. are the more integrate steps.
Yet...First we start with basic cleaning in our daily life, or preparation for the chakra balancing....
If we want to take our self to a higher possibility we first need to purify, cleanse our physical body, rip the negative energy off.
No matter which option you choose there is always a short meditation* involved:
Take three deep breaths, then focus on pureness and clear energy, breathe it in and exhale gently passing the renewed energy from your lungs into your blood stream.
If we are familiar with Reiki we can combine Reiki through time and space, "Hon sha se sho nen," three times we pull the pure white light toward us and linger a moment in inner peace, "Sei he ki."

A wind bath

- When the going gets tough, walk outside in a storm. You will feel more transparent as if a layer is ripped off. *Meditate.

A water bath

- If you don't have the sea close by, shower at home with sea salt. Rub it all over the body. Give yourself a massage with the salt, and do the short meditation standing in the shower, optional is sending light to the people you touched. Then shower with the usual soap and feel freer.
  When you let water run over your skin, the layer around you is washed off as well.

A fire bath

- Place 5 candles around you and sit in meditation during 30 minutes.
- Take an incense stick and pass all around your body, or ask somebody you trust to do this to you, so you can close your eyes. *Meditate.

A sand/mud bath

- On the beach you put the wet sand of the shore on your skin, then feel the sunlight upon your skin a moment, *meditate, be aware you are releasing the energies and enter the sea and to wash it off.

Chakra cleansing

Each method is found here in this book

- Prayer
- Meditation
- Reiki or touching of the hand
- Comprehension of the power of each chakra and uplifting it through mental imprints and affirmations.

Karmic cleansing

is done through complex processes that involve comprehension of what affects us, forgiveness letter written by hand, release rituals are most effective during an eclipse. Astral travel sessions with a good healer or life coach may be recommended here as well, since usually the karma is installed before the actual time.

Seeing the aura field

Along my path of life, other than my daughter, I met only one person who could see the aura in people through the most unusual circumstances possible. During my initiation ceremony as shaman in Monterrey, the north of Mexico, I found him.

One of the shamans that formed the sacred circle around me fascinated me completely; he was blind. Alfredo was his birth name. I've never seen anybody so joyous and free. The most amazing thing about him was his look. He totally penetrated my being. I've never felt so naked in front of anybody.

At some point, he spoke my name and came straight at me. I was puzzled because I was sitting by myself and had not spoken, so he could not have recognized my voice. With an "I have conquered the world" smile on his face, he said that my inner light had a unique warm brightness, which distinguished me from the rest and made me easily recognizable in a crowd full of people.

You can imagine how my enthusiasm was rising to its maximum capacity and how I've bombarded him with questions. He was such a fascinating being! He explained that about seven years ago, his wife opened his third eye in a ritual. She always spoke of "invisible to the eye" beings, and he had doubted her words like most of us do when people talk about angels or spirit guides. After an accident in his childhood, his world became dark, eyes closed or open. He remembers vaguely the forms of mountains, trees, people, and cars. The day his wife put him through the ritual, nothing changed for him, so a little disappointed, he went to the movies in the evening with her. Another thing I was fascinated about was the incredible dedication of his wife. With her indications about the sceneries, he had enough imagination to enjoy listening to a movie to be able to follow it.

When suddenly he asked her, "Why did they switch such a bright light on?" she knew what that meant and smiled because the light of God had once again gained over darkness. She answered, to his amazement, that the theater was in complete darkness. Then suddenly in his inner vision, colors and shapes appeared. He cried of such beauty and tried to capture it all as long as possible, thinking it would disappear again just like how his actual vision had also vanished. But it stayed with him as a gift unwrapped. He did some investigation and understood he was able to see the aura and the inner light of the people around him. His sixth sense was fully activated, the intuition or pituitary gland. Some call this the third eye. His wife lost her abilities to see the spirit world from that very moment. It's like she passed her gift on to him. He has expanded and increased this special ability now, seven years later, to the fullest. He can perceive people's colors over the phone, indicating how they are feeling, in order to help them through trials and difficult moments.

I asked Alfredo how he saw me. He told me my inner light was very bright and pure, while the colors around me constantly changed during the ceremony according to how I was feeling. But not one moment did my inner light decrease its strength. He gave me one of the most important messages a human being had ever given me, explaining that a pure light cannot be affected by outside influences or emotions. The only way I can harm myself is by denying to feel the light. This is where I understand how the ethereal body works and how meditation increases and benefits our overall health, wellness mood, and, as a consequence, our success in life.

I was happy to finally see all the channelings I received confirmed by somebody very wise and trustworthy. Till then my only source of information was the inner spirit world and I did my best all those years to believe it. Now I knew I could trust my inner self ☺

I remember that my first reaction after seeing Alfredo was that I felt sorry for him. But after hearing him speak, I admired him and almost felt sorry for people who have their outer vision activated. I cannot always feel my light within, nor give it priority. We're very distracted by what our eyes see, analyzing and judging instead of going within and looking at the essence of all that is. I feel we waste a lot of valuable time.

But I can say that ever since I met him, I spend more time in silence. I enjoy my eyesight more. I feel grateful to be able to see sunsets, the morning light, the colors of birds, and flowers. When it rains in the night and the morning fog hangs over the forest, I enjoy the spider webs and the first rays of sunlight penetrating the branches. Then I stop and breathe the fresh air in, absorbing the smell of the pines and feeling the morning sun upon my face and embracing my cells in love.

The combination of the shaman-initiating ceremony and the union with Alfredo purified and intensified my inner light. And from then on, I could feel people from within and sort of "scan" a person, the ability to read between the lines, or take the inner sunglasses off. Fakeness was being captured instantly by my being, and I usually caressed the person, saying they could stop trying to impress me or convince me that they were worth loving. I saw, from then on, their true being and have shocked many with that clear vision. And besides, I had been an expert in "makeup, high heels, perfect outfits" cover-ups to hide my inner pain; so smiles, bulldog attitudes, and fancy impressions couldn't fool me any longer.

The four layers of brainwaves

Become your own best friend

The four brain wave stages define how we feel. It is very subtle and requires a person to be truly focused if you'd love to know which brain wave you're on. And, as you may have noticed, theta is really hard to reach when we're on "on-going".
Nature walks, creative actions, enthusiastic reactions help us remain on "alpha", in the more peaceful, empowering state of being. I explain all about inner communication in this book —active and passive meditations—, so you can enjoy the theta wave and discover that your best friend resides within, and is always at reach.

- **Delta**: a state of —unaware— higher consciousness connection, during most part of our life achieved only in deep, peaceful sleep.
- **Theta**: and embracive feeling, consciously, to belong, to have purpose, to feel powerful, to be part of a creative energy and a sense to be "lighter" than the human body feels like.
- **Alpha**: we have the feeling to be strong, to be able to manipulate our events in a positive and productive way, we feel free and satisfied.
- **Beta**: we are in a state of action, very much alert. And this state has a "good productive layer" but it is like living on the edge, because stress and anxiety can be triggered easily if we can't switch at will to alpha.

Important to know: any thought or idea we repeat more than 5 times in our thoughts become part of our conscious mind as if it's "ours".

With this sequence of brainwaves in mind I present to you after this story, the circle of aliveness and how we as human beings move through the entire process and need to experience challenges, with the opportunity to activate "choice" and not feel victim of circumstances.

In order to heal oneself or reach others we need to learn to enter the theta brainwave state. The theta level is where we can truly reach through time and space. The next story is one of my most powerful examples I can offer you related to how this inner connection can manifest itself and how it can benefit those we love.

It is mastery level, yet it is very humane as well.

Get Up, Dad

Is there a possibility to work through distance, healing others? That was a question I was confronted with often in conversations. The answer is yes. The how is hard for me to explain. I know how to tune in to others, yet I feel I am having a hard time explaining the exact mechanism of the how we actually feel each other, trespassing time/space.

I was writing in my cabin at 11 a.m. Suddenly, I felt an incredible pain in my chest, and a vision of my dad suffering like he was in his last minutes of life came. I grabbed my phone and wanted to dial his number, but I also knew I was incapable of speaking in that moment. I was suffocated by pain and fear. My dad was "going," and I didn't get a chance to tell him how wonderful he actually was. I wrote him a text message. It took me a lot longer than usual due to the fact that tears came streaming down constantly and my hands were shaking so much I made many mistakes. Finally, I got my message through, about how he is a dear friend to me, how much I love him and appreciate all the effort he had done in his life to be able to offer me the education and support he had given, and added that the past was forgiven and absorbed by love itself. When I pressed Send, I sat still for a long time in silence, sending healing love and affection, and slowly, I became more at ease.

A few minutes earlier in Belgium, my dad had fallen on the ground while working on his vegetable garden located one mile from our house. A stroke. Receiving my words with the sound of the incoming message signal, he grabbed his phone with his last strength and read my words. Ignited with love, he called my mom and asked for an ambulance. Ten minutes later, he was on his way to the hospital and under the capable hands of a specialist. My mom called me hours later 'cause my dad had asked her to thank me.

I took a plane to visit him, and when he saw me, he asked, "How did you know?"

My answer was, "I love you."

Therapists, instructors, managers, nurses, teachers, dentists, you took an oath similar to mine. Daily, at least six times a day, we absorb people's weight. The fact is that I'm aware that I said, "I want to be a channel for good," a powerful affirmation imprinted upon my DNA; my openness is of a large scale. But we're all linked, one with the other, through our inner energy system whether we're aware of it or not.

So we really need to take time to reencounter balance daily. It can be through Reiki, meditations, temazcal, yoga or tai chi classes, sauna, or a bath in the sea.

Some people's energies are very heavy. It can even take us days to let go of them.

Besides professionally connected, when we're sensitive, we're linked up very close to our loved ones. When our children are at school and they're having a tough problem, we might feel acid in our stomach; when our partner is working and feels stress, our head might start feeling pressure. Also, each discussion with someone we love settles down in the lower belly/back, one of the emotional chakras. Or the mother-daughter issues settle in the breast area. Instantly take some deep breaths, doing the same statements that we do in the shower with salt; send light to our loved ones. Focus on pureness. Focus on clean energy. Breathe all that in. Concentrate deeply, and be willing to release beyond any doubt. The more you practice, the better you get.

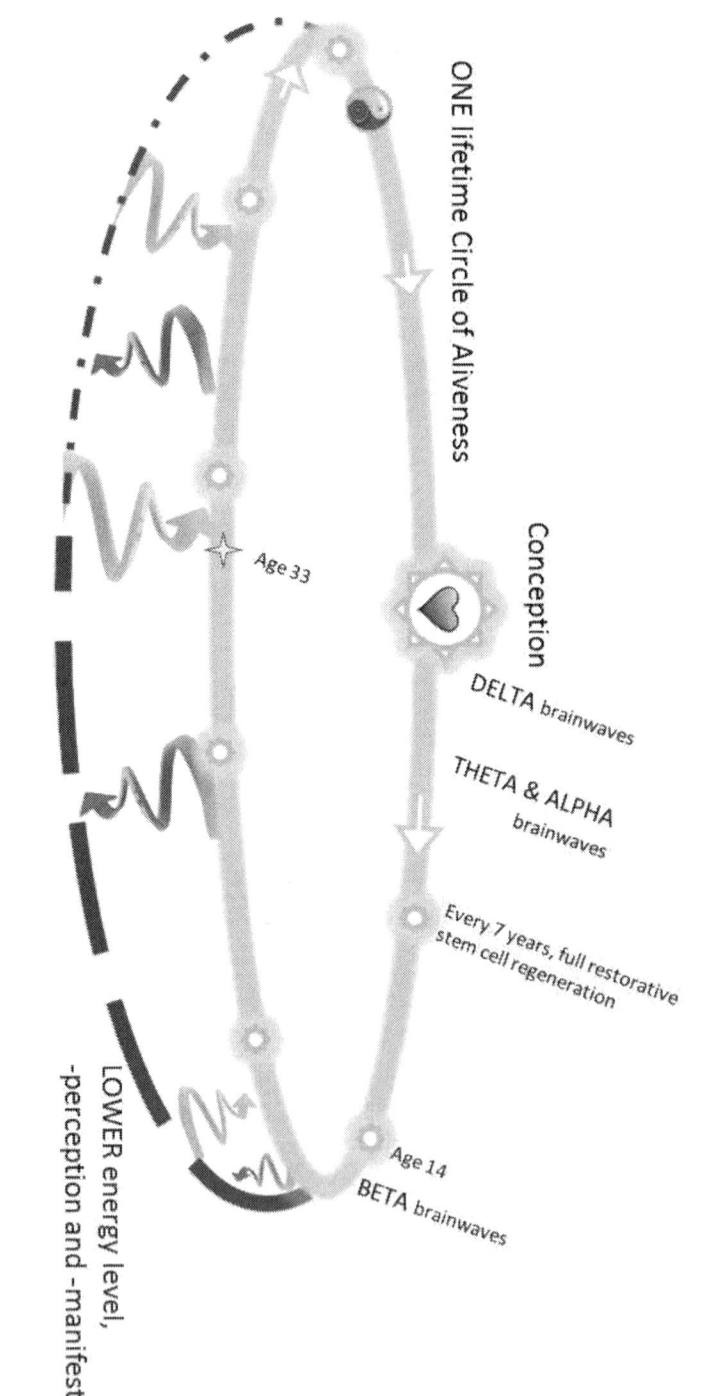

The green line of ALIVENESS

At the moment of conception we carry the divine imprint "that we can be powerful, free, happy, healthy, fulfilled, successful and affluent.
Tools are given to us: "free will" and a choice to live in the resonance of "compassion and being grateful".
I call this the circle of aliveness.
Let's say, "a green life-line" is created.

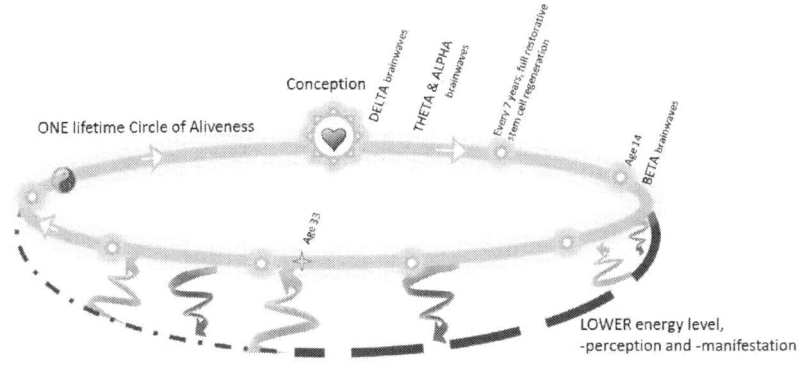

Stage 1. We are in the realm of the higher consciousness as a baby in the womb of our mom, within the delta brain wave state. And at birth, when we enter into the light and air of the earth plane, we lower one level of "waves" and remain in between the theta and alpha waves during some time; up to —maximum— 7 years of age. Our green line is our "playground", having a constant inner communication with "home", the divine collective consciousness. Each chakra is therefore fully connected.
One of our main attributes we can use as a tool in this life is FREE WILL.
Between the age of five and seven we start questioning authority, habits,.. we take control from a logic point of view, lower our perception, with that lessen our energy intake and automatically shift to the "active brainwaves". Our chakras are no longer working on 100% reception of energy, because we associate most of our experiences from the earth plane's points of view, which are more limited than our original imprint.

Age fourteen: another alteration.

Each person shifts to the beta brainwave state. It is programmed this way in our human evolution in order to experience all levels of existing and activate FREE WILL.

We start living in highs and lows. Reaching the alpha or theta brain waves on certain occasions, like on Christmas or on our birthday, yet since on many of the other moments we start calculating, fearing, doubting, lingering in disappointment, we slowly move further away from our original power. In that process the red line is formed! Creating the feeling of being lost at times, extremely confused and most definitely not comprehended by those who surround us.

So the red line/zone is actually a temporarily state teaching us how uncomfortable it is to live in it, since it is basically an accumulation of negative thoughts and counter-productive behaviors. Dependent people in general are unaware how much they are breaking themselves down; at least 80% of their conscious thoughts are about worrying, doubting, blaming or wanting to change the past.

We do have a choice, since this red line-state is just a challenge.

So, don't fear for your loved ones; every single person also has the "ascension process" activated at the same time. The "free will" to return, by activating the higher brain waves, any time.

And as an extra gift, every seven years our chakras, by being connected to their original source, enhance again pure energy and our stem cells are restored fully. Each organ in our system benefits, if we can comprehend this process, we can use it during those next seven years continuously. The intelligent imprint upon our stem cells reproduces itself automatically if we "co-operate" and recognize its divinity. This is where free will comes in; do we wish to remain healthy and peaceful, or do we choose to go through the trials human life offers? The key lies into being aware of the 7 chakras, raise the brain-wave level and see the opportunities in life, and think from the highest capacity possible.

Another gift! With the age of 33 —age of the Christ— each human being has the chance to raise the vibration to the theta level and open the inner portal. Happiness is lived within your safe space, with short intense heights and in general a satisfying daily life and peaceful nights.

All emotions need to be experienced along our life, in order to grow and establish "detachment and free will". Short lapses of being angry, frustrated or sad doesn't make you leave your green line, unless you can't remain in control and start feeling victim.

Remember....there is only one thing that can kill our success: thoughts and feelings based on doubt, fear and uncertainties.

Each time we repeat, in our head, somebody's insult or low-leveled vison, we are affirming that "that vision or insult" is part of who we are. More than five thoughts take us into the "red zone".

Trouble puts us on the edge, and from that edge we can choose if we will detach and move on, or if we would like to "eat the trouble for breakfast, lunch and dinner, if it will blur all our sunny moments from then on". If so, we enter the red zone and our emotional body, then physical body will pay the price.

I suggest to each human being to build a garden upon your green line,.. convert the " thin line" that seems like a ridge, into a "large safe space where trust, faith, believe and hope flows" where we don't feel no longer vulnerable, instead create a sacred orchard filled with certainties that can be recuperated, restored, reproduced and embraced freely.

In short...The green line personality is the innocence and openness of a free spirited child in combination with a mature serene passionate adult. The red line is anything that disturbs your true self or distracts your true self from living its potential.

The next information is for those who wish to go more in depth...

Shedding more light on the aliveness chart

Until the age of 14 we have that burning desire to do things right and to impress our family and teachers.
For most of us, at first we "left" our safety zone (green line), were eager to find more respect. We started moving downward into the spiral towards the red zone. In the beginning, once in a while we still entered voluntarily into our peaceful, embracive space. But most of us were bullied or not comprehended, so we grew further and further away from feeling "embraced and respected". Over the next years, it became a quest to search for self-love and success in anything we pursued. Our ideals shifted and our vision became more "earthy" and we became very independent and determent to 'gain respect somehow'.
At a certain point along our life we started to believe again in abundance, peace and immeasurable love, imprinted upon our memory-cellular system, and we choose to remain as long as possible upon the green zone. If when we may feel anxious or live a deep trauma, through outside influence, we no longer dwell upon the effects, but choose to regain the feeling of empowerment.
We shift priorities.
We side-track easily. There are a lot of distractions we can fall in before we reach the green line. And if we would engage in them, it is important to know that we can't linger in them.
7 times in our life, all the stem cells are changed, aiding our organs. We have the opportunity to make changes on our DNA; repairing and embracing the past, enlightening our future path.
At the age of 49, after 7 imprinted purifications, we the choice to continue upon this healthy and balanced way of life, and will know how to apply all the tools during our last stage of life. We will live rich, virtuous and age in a light and youthful way, our intellect is raised towards a higher consciousness and we take constantly wise decisions.
But sadly enough, those who ignore the presented opportunities and with the age of 49 they have not been able to choose through free will to return into their true self and encounter self-love, heavy challenges overwhelm them, and they may live their last years of life in physical, emotional, and mental suffering, in resentment blaming others, linger in loneliness,.. grumpy old people.

While reading this chapter, it seems as if we don't stand a chance for success, but actually what happens is that success is guaranteed if only we can come out of that victimhood feeling. Our success and fulfillment depends upon our capacity to believe in ourselves and to stand our ground when others doubt us or dictate our life. Some, with the age of 18 can already come out and rise up, others fall in addiction and despair during several years.
Sport or art are powerful enhancements to establish inner balance and minimize the inner confused or lost-feelings during those challenging times.

Imaginary vision of a purification process

Envision a natural spring filled with the attributes of the 7 chakras. As the water starts flowing, it becomes a stream and along its path it is being influenced and manipulated, until that precious water contains pollution.
Yet, if we can believe in the power of nature....the river itself has the key to purify the water again; the rocks laying in the stream cleanse the added-on pollution, until we have the same pureness and quality, with added-on wisdom obtained from the experiences.

Our personal gifted chakra

As Soul and Spirit we are a light being.
We have access to several vibration consciousness planes to which we can travel to any time throughout the power of intention which activates the shift in experience.
Our soul home base: Envision a cosmic dance of colorful lights. We change colors and can travel with them to different planes.
On the Causal planes we're able to enjoy to the fullest our creative capacity. Transform ourselves in animals, waterfalls, rainbows, human forms who eat fruit formed at will instantly.
On the Astral planes we enter usually after returning from a lower plane like the earth for instance to appreciate again the gifts of the universe. Like the opening of a flower. The metamorphose of a butterfly. Honey

from a bee. Cows. Clouds. Sunsets. The white sand on a beach. The colors before a storm on the ocean. The astral planes are very much like the earth,..only the negative energies are missing. Mastery can be imprinted again to use in later experiences, when we return to earth.

When we come to earth with the color of our choice we live experiences, challenges, a mission, a strength and a weakness to conquer. Our entire life is interdependently in synch with this 'color'. Every decision of expansion is correlated to our source. This color is called 'our gifted chakra' it is a link which is in constant union. There is a perfect balance on earth in order for each soul to expand in Light. Our needs are met. Encounters are understood.

Our Gifted Chakra —CG in short, Chakra Gift
are covering the 4 basic needs on earth
1. Success, abundance, self-esteem up, confident, related to the second chakra.
2. Inner child aliveness, creativity, related to the third chakra
3. Patience, compassion, tolerance, comprehension, related to the fourth chakra
4. Expression of our needs, communication and release, related to the fifth chakra.

Please understand we have bits and parts of each chakra activated. But you will recognize only 'one' as the one that stands out in most of the situations in life, and has survived every 'storm'. Where do you see your strongest link?

This cannot be calculated by date of birth, it can only be recognized through a stem cell reading, since that is where this information is stored..

If you wish to have the affirmation on yours, feel free to approach me on one of my conferences, classes or workshops, or write to my e-mail "sandra8mallorca@gmail.es".

A person becomes more powerful though time and experience. I have understood that people experience 7 life times in each group, in order to perfect it each time. When somebody entered the cycle they are vulnerable, but as soon as they have achieved certainties, they are true masters within the game of life.

I am clearly a 3rd chakra gifted person. Ups and downs very clearly marked, innovative, inner child activated and a constant need to be creative and productive in channeling. I love teaching others how to be successfully creative as well.

I am clearly in one of my last life times in this number, because I really feel powerful in each aspect, and in the ones I am weaker, I can take full priority to become stronger in them, which is not perfection in outcome,. .it is perfection in potential. I always live my own maximum capacity.

Family and friends harmony

We can comprehend, learn to live in harmony with each other, appreciate and learn from one another thanks to the fact that there are four different kinds of people, according to a perfect plan. 'Perfectly dis functional families' teach us the best way of survival, strength and how stand up for yourself. If we would just stop blaming our family for our circumstances, we'd see the opportunities for growth and maturity.

What couples concern, it can be useful to know your partner's gifted chakra, to accept them the way they are and aid them in expanding in light and live, so they can feel fulfilled. A fulfilled male partner, comes home with a smile and is free to enjoy the evening with us. Keeps the stud muffin alive, doesn't it! Either way, if the wife is feeling good in her job, she keeps on seeing her partner as a delicious piece of pie, if she's disappointed in her job, she just wants a foot massage and point!

Our task is to enhance the life quality in every person we touch, within our gifted capacity.

Didn't we all experience the feeling that people use us only for a certain determent purpose, and as soon as they achieve that which they pursued, they move on. And we felt insulted by those unjust treatments. Sometimes it takes a season, sometimes it is even a shorter encounter.

Well, it happens constantly, because it is meant to be so.

We tend to second CG's when we're in need of a counselor on the how to be more successful in a certain area of our life. Their presence sometimes makes us take already a different attitude in life. For instance, as third CG person I write, compose fabulous work, but I need a manager to bring it to the public.

People turn to us, third CG's when they're in need to have some more creativity, light heartedness and fun

Heart chakra gifted are those who embrace their kids, offer gifts, and by seeing it we become more loving. We go to them to be heard. We can talk to them about our heart desires and they have the patience to listen to us without no judgment.

And the fifth CG person is attended when we need intellectual support, a new computer, a quick solution to a problem. They are the experts who know the details and save us from having to read the manuals. They have invested their time already. Perfect uncles or aunts. A some distance, yet always at our disposal if we have an issue or a problem to solve, or when we need a higher point of view.

Please see it from 'above' how the sum of the 4 gifts would create a fully functional society. Each person having its share, and harmony would flow. Life on earth would be a great place. We constantly meet up with each other's needs. The great thing would be, if we would all greet, not with our name and job, 'I am Pedro, accountant', but 'I am Pedro and I am second chakra gifted, I work as accountant. how about you?' Instantly we would see what the other person can offer us, the message behind the encounter, and benefit us to the maximum.

Can you see how once we live our mission is it is so much easier to enter in a meditative state and find inner stillness. And how restlessness ceases to push us forward.

Whatever your mission is keep clear in your mind that sometimes in a room filled with people there are many ears to hear, but no real hearing takes place.

Humanity has a defensive system rooted which prevent them from seeing the benefits of 'growth'. While growing up, each one of us has been hurt.'

Right after writing this channeled information, I opened the inner conversation and said to my higher self….

- I understand now, where were you when I needed you before in my life?!

'You were in the room filled with people who have 'physical' ears.'

- If I could only be 'aware' or have enough faith to trust in you when you reach out to me..........

'You have, you are. So far you haven't disappointed me; only yourself.'

As Adults

Second chakra gifted, CG

- Appear in people's life for a very short amount if time. They help us take that one step up.
- Examples, incredibly skilled sport athletes.
- You can see them from far because they take care of their body as a priority.
- Natural born leaders in the business market.
- They select the time they spend with people, having a tight schedule.
- They are strong people. Very determent, and persistent if they've set a goal.
- Solid rocks in society.
- We find them on our path when we're in need to be successful.
- They have the capacity to create confidence in a person in a short amount of time, but they are very selective what close friends concern. When you get a chance to be close friends with one of the second chakra people, means you've somehow conquered his heart, which he/she only reserves for their nearest family normally.
- They love to be around intelligent people who still teach them important values in life.
- Their mission is to help others professionally, show them the path and means to success, but then need to redraw so their 'students' can be successful through choice and firm steps, not led by their masters hand. They can not become dependent upon them.

- So, since they stay only short amount of time, appearing 'for one single reason', they feel lonely sometimes, which they have learned to avoid with working harder.
- Very high reproduction capacity. Strong believers in abundance.
- They place the ladder very high for themselves, yet still manage to be outstanding in the quality of their work.

Third chakra gifted

- We are so sensitive, that we can tune into the stem cells of others. We know innate that we are all one. Our system knows.
- Careful here though!
- It is a gift that we can see the potential of people but take it personal when our loved ones don't want to live up to it. Union oriented. We are one.
- We ache for truth, we need to be with people who are honest and open to us, or we die. The pain is so much that we get sick.
- Decision taking is tough for us, we see the future visions of our maximum potential. In my personal case, I take decisions according to it. But since I am not very advanced yet in comprehending the visions. Sometimes they are an indication is what I need to prepare myself for, but it can take years before I have evolved towards my potential to be able to live the manifestation of the vision.
- We have the biggest challenge ahead being a single mother.
- Our sensitivity makes us irritated when several notices mix, or constant shouting of kids gets on our nerves
- We're extremely spontaneous, and can shock people sometimes.
- The inner child seeks approval from the parent, acting immature sometimes. We keep the cord to the parents active, until we change that cord for the silver cord to our higher self.

Isn't that great knowledge?! Gosh, why didn't I know this before in my life. Every action, decision was based on achievement to be loved and applauded by my dad. As soon as we have SELF esteem, we don't need somebody exterior to tell us how well we're doing.

- Confidence in myself is fully activated now in me. My second chakra is open, backing up my mission, which is the third chakra.
- We become alive at night after a few hours of sleep, or in the early morning, inspired by creativity, like a fountain that keeps on offering water. It asks to by used wisely, paid attention to. So we work at the most impossible hours, and often are tired, up to exhaustion in the daytime. In the night we find the stillness that is needed to perceive the cosmic creative realms. Most of us, third and fourth CG's fall asleep early, and need some romantic or peaceful 'un pluck' relaxing movie time before falling asleep,. While second and fifth love to stay up late and work.
- My ups are of such freedom and aliveness expression that I breathe bubbles instead of air. When I am balanced I can see beauty in a raindrop hanging on a leaf, stop right there and then, and enjoy the moment to the fullest. I can go to the movies and penetrate the scenes as though I am part of it, I laugh, cry with profound sadness and feel the writer's personal path through the entire movie.
- I create very profound friendships, close bonds with people in no time.
- Whenever I am treated with 'injustice' I loose a grip on this balance and confusion takes over. I become defensive like a wounded animal and aggressive when people keep on stabbing in it. I had a tendency to take things personal.
- In order for me to find balance I need to enter in silence often, breathe conscious so the innocent lightness in me can stay activated.
- Keep on offering myself the opportunity to live happy moments. Get out there, do things without expectations. I am like a child who needs action, friends, love, encouragement and I can recognize my 'attributes' in many of you.
- I can see third gifted people from far. We are the center piece of a room, we are the ones who create atmosphere and

ambiance when everybody is caught up in stressful and worried thoughts. We awaken people's inner child, generally in a brilliant and unique way, sometimes by our example.
- Most of the time, the spark in our eyes ignites people's aliveness.
- We own a 'free being- walking style'.
- Only when we're under heavy burdens or hardship, do we tend to bent forward for some time. But we always find our 'firm posture' back.
- We ignite creativity, inspire people to stay enthusiastic, spontaneous.
- When people meet us, they are in need to allow their inner child to be more playful in their private time, and/or become more prosper in a way where they enjoy their professional life again. Each of us have a different way of projecting this message.
- We use art as a portal. Art portals are found where we least expect it, weaving a basket, painting, singing in the shower, walking the dog,.. It is in anything and every unique place on earth where you realize you've stopped thinking and just relaxed your entire being. Creative present moments embraced. Art in the eye of the beholder, love in the precious intent of its creator.
People who are in practice of creating art, may it be in music, painting, writing,.. are in the 'zone'. absorbed by it, submerged in it. A great and precious portal which is a fantastic way to offer your loving contribution to society and earn a living.

I've come a long way in self-discovery since the first time I learned about the 3rd chakra: inner child awake. Many years have passed but I realize this child in me is only increasing in power, due to the fact I cleaned traumas and karma from my life, so my inner child can play in freedom.
The character John Coffey in The Green Mile represents 100% a third chakra gifted person. His words speak for us...

> "I'm rightly tired of the pain I hear and feel, boss. I'm tired of bein on the road, lonely as a robin in the rain. Not never havin no buddy to go on with or tell me where we's comin from or goin to or why. I'm tired of people bein

ugly to each other. It feels like pieces of glass in my head. I'm tired of all the times I've wanted to help and couldn't. I'm tired of bein in the dark. Mostly it's the pain. There's too much. If I could end it, I would. But I can't."

— Stephen King, The Green Mile

Fourth chakra gifted

- Their priority is set towards love.
- They are not as ambitious as the rest of us, very laid back until they see the benefits, how many people's hearts they get to touch.
- 100% open hearted giving people, the people who keep true compassion and empathy alive on earth.
- Very considerate and cautious with the way they express themselves.
- Love is wisdom expressed in its purest form. They can surprise us with such intelligent remarks, because the essence of their words is love.
- Success is measured by them with how well their family is doing.
- They always walk that extra mile for their family and close friends, thinking about ways how to please others, forgetting about themselves often.
- They should practice more workouts, take walks, sport classes, because they have the tendency to take on 'the weight of others' and then feel lazy and heavy, eating more than needed.
- They hardly have thoughts, worries or future plans. In general they are very peaceful within. On the other hand, they are more inclined to have opinions, which influence their entire behavior and determine their near future.
- Their only struggle is that they accumulate self worth through giving, caring, nurturing, and their challenge lies in the moment their children have reached the age to leave the nest, they feel lost, and can enter in victim state when they don't find self love, have a hobby or other friendships.

- Tele novels touch a sweet spot in them. They love to know the stories of the entire neighborhood. Are over concerned for them. In short you could say, they don't really own a life of their own.
- Giving is what makes them be alive. They have no sense of possession at all. Yet one trap: they often feel left out. When there is a family union or party, the heart chakra gifted person will do all the cooking, will be doing the dishes, which she believes it is her task to do so,.yet inside of her she wishes it weren't so. Deep inside herself she feels victim of that situation. In the 'need any help?' answer they give lies their evolvement. On their path lies the opportunity to live in the center between the giving and the taking. Their true task on earth is to give of the heart, but in order to get over victim hood, then need to learn to receive the gifts people offer. From strangers and close family.
- In order to be prosper. f you have a family member who is a four, guide them by expanding their view of 'family', social worker, projects where the heart is involved, where compassion flows as empathy among the people involved.

In my yoga class we work circle wise. Always. That's when I distinguish the fourth chakra gifted easily. They usually take distance, right out of the circle and then I actually need to pull them in so they take up their rightful place!

Fifth chakra gifted

- Super intelligent
- I'll see it when I believe it
- They take a certain health habit only if they have seen the proof of it. If they have received all the information and it is tested by them. Very resistant to take old habits out.
- Punctual, correct, hyper responsible
- Gives powerful mind blowing clues to us, hidden in funny remarks, or even in cynical expressions. Life solutions are hidden in the answers they give when you ask them a simple question.
- Solitary leaders
- Need prestige, be seen

- They tend to use the intelligence to know all the details of all the products they want to buy. Detail freaks. They want to be informed and dominate it.
- They compare themselves to others, often copy other people to obtain attention. Are skilled actors.
- They dream about a simple, laid back kind of life, early retirement, after investing long work hours now today, enjoy later. But they keep on postponing that laid back in time moment...for a later moment.
- Loves to work long hours, feeling useful until the very last moment before closing their eyes.
- They are so negative and lost in lack of achievement while they are on the red line, that their loved ones need to learn to avoid them, in order to stay unattached by their side.
- Through constant thriving, persistence and achieving, they found out they can make things happen. This is different than a second chakra, who are innate successful people, effortless.
- They need freedom.
- They need to be the ones who take decisions for everything they do, they can not be forced, or told to do something. When they choose to do something, they are truly powerful and successful.
- As kids, they are very independent and way too smart for their age.
- The earth is a very heavy vibration to them, they loose themselves often in daydreaming.
- They are very psychic and intuitive, yet their wisdom is not always felt by others, cause not everybody can tune into that fine vibration tone of intelligence. For 'others' it takes sometimes a long time before they(we) can capture the true meaning of their words and work with it.
- Their vibration is so thin they can be in a room without being noticed. What they most fear is for their real value not to be known by others. They'll walk that extra mile to help their friends, and when they're not with self confident enough, they need to be recognized and applauded for it.

- They have difficulties adjusting to the system, since the system is boring and limited.
- When they choose to be, they are very warmhearted and tender, yet only when they trust their partner. They scan you first to see if you're a worthy partner. Being in love doesn't 'happen' to them, they permit themselves to love the person who passed the test.
- They have the capacity to sense the sentence you're about to say and anticipate giving you the solution to your problem before you have even pronounced it.
- Their difficulty lies in 'not releasing' and live often in remorse. They can linger a long time in regret or they take years to let go of something that happened. Being hard with those who harmed them at a certain point.
- Feeling satisfied lasts only a few moments, if they feel it at all. They are constantly thriving for more. On and on.
- They live short lasting passions, high lights which fade slowly until it feels to them like an obligation. That's where depression enters their system, provoking 'sense of' lack of productivity.
- Towards the public they always seem light hearted, easy going and very fear- dominant, yet they can be very frustrated and impatient when nobody's watching.
- They hold the key to reach our higher self in daily life. They are here to communicate us that which we can't see for ourselves. When they appear in our lives is because we are ready to be more of who we are. Trust me, your life will be upside down in no time, yet after some time balance and a unique connection to your inner self is the gift.

Did you ever watch the funny movie Turner and Hooch with Tom Hanks. The character he plays is a typical fifth chakra gifted person. The five writers who wrote the screenplay knew exactly out of personal experience how it is to live and deal with such a person. How to bring the best out of him.

Once they commit to someone or something they are the greatest most dedicated and sweet people possible. But until they do...like the song from Maná says it is easier to touch the sun than to reach his heart, 'es mas facil llegar al sol que a tu corazon.' And that's the truth about a fifth chacra person. They just don't let you in. And if they do, but you make one mistake, you'll find the main door with an extra lock. Tree mistakes, the sign 'do not disturb' will be up 24/7. And it takes them somewhere between a decade and a century to forgive you.

What if it the encounter and relationship is meant to be? Is it worth it? It's a hell of a struggle, and a lot of giving in for a third CG like me. Every move they make is calculated, while we feed ourselves with enthusiastic spontaneous actions.

Everything they own is the highest quality possible.

And we, as partners really need to evolve to our highest potential and then we can have true harmony with them, and lead them into a life filled with shared moments of quality.

> I was writing at dawn in my cabin and Indyra, age 7 then, came to my bed like she did every morning, only this time her hair was more disordered than usual.
>
> 'I had a dream mammy...I was a baby horse and you were a mammy horse. We were running in the fields together.'
>
> 'Oh really, that's beautiful' I responded and meanwhile I started to tap with my fingers one by one on my laptop, like the sound of a horse running in gallop. I asked her to join me, and she tapped with all her fingers together. So I told her to take only one finger at a time, slowly.
>
> She looked straight at me saying 'But mammy. The baby horse never learned to walk slowly. The mammy horse ran very quick and the baby needed to learn to run with its 4 legs together to be able to stay with the mammy'.

I suddenly realized I had a challenge ahead!

I don't know about you, but while I'm head deep in the inside of a perception I usually act selfishly ignorant towards other approaches or points of view.

Right after Indy's birth, when we were at home the first weeks, I remember thinking. 'Oh Lord, she is so fragile! She depends on me fully, I am responsible for her. I can't fail!' I was a single parent, her father left us one week before her birth.

And remembering my own childhood I felt threatened by the fearful, loneliness and lost feelings I experienced when I was growing up, so being aware of all the traps we can fall in as a child, I was determent to give her an opportunity to maintain emotional stability, health, freedom and fulfillment feeling. I wanted to be a balanced person and mom, left the known behind and retreated in the wild for three years.

At first when I had the transformation done, the inner connection established with myself, I felt free,...my yoga classes, conferences and one on one sessions became a warm hearted expression and a blessed safe haven for me and all those I touched. Feeling grateful to be able to tap with my conscious intellect in daily life into the Higher Consciousness.

But along all of this I was totally blind, unaware that I was becoming a control freak upon my close relationships. Committing life mistakes in what mattered the most. How could this be happening to me, a person who preaches about peace, with 40.000 people a month from all over the planet reading my website on emotional stability, chakras, soul mates, tantra,.

And it wasn't until now, when my daughter needed a few months by herself, me that I asked my best friend what exactly I was doing to make people take distance from me. He told me I was the most selfish person he had ever known. Talking about a reality check. All I was aware of is that I was nervous around them, up to a point of insecure and filled with anxiety, but I each time put the blame on me not being experienced with close relationships or on them, not acting 'proper' accorded to my vision of happiness. But yeah,.. I see the entire picture now.

I shall tell you in a bit the entire 'love story' about the man I feel to be my life partner. Last year, when he needed 'space', I grew a 14x9 ovarian cyst not being able to handle the distance, emotionally drained. And this influenced my relationship with my daughter, I became unstable and she wasn't used to see her mom in pain or 'down'.

I had strict rules with her and usually they didn't feel heavy because I had always been able to be light hearted and 'a funny adventurous mom', but the emotional pain was overwhelming. And my happiness and respecting codes of honor suddenly became a heaviness upon her, because I was constantly nagging about it.

What the bleep do you know, the law of attraction, the teachings of Dr Emoto, how water is influenced,...pushed me even more to 'remain on the straight path'. And the 'Don't do this! Be careful!'...echoed in her ears non stop around the clock.

Through constant pressure, the heat builds up inside and inevitably someday the precious mountain becomes an erupting volcano, burning everything we build up. Yet I have faith that the lava touching the soil knows that my intention was pure and filled with loving and enlightening knowledge and how to maintain the wisdom active as well,.. and new life, more balanced this time, can grow stronger.

What if we dedicate our life seeking for the perfect flower, and with our last breath we realize 'They are all perfect!' Will you join me on the quest to 'recognizing LIFE in every single breath'.

Kids
trials, and high lights

Second CG
- Are successful, talented and are followed by the others of the class or group.
- Sport athletes, and team leaders.
- Trial: they are envied. By students and often when the teachers are imbalanced, also by the adults who teach them. They are so certain of themselves that they shock them with their young powerful identity.
- They should not pick the glove up. People will keep on challenging them. Some will even try to break their strong will.
- They stay powerful warriors, in loyalty, dignity and justice if they don't participate in the competition that others take on in life.

Third CG
- Our feelings are so sensitive it becomes a vulnerability in our youth. Every unjust touch against us can leave heavy marks. We see the potential of a sweet, strong dad, and when he doesn't respects us, it leaves deep wounds in us. These wounds bring us

out of our source center and can lead to loneliness and lost many many years.
- We are all over the place, many needs, changing like the wind, yet very loyal and determent to achieve goals
- Very enthusiastic and eager to be respected, comprehended and most of us love to be in the spotlight.

Fourth CG
- Internally sensitive vulnerable to opinions and critics, not showing the reactions they have upon those opinions from others, they keep it hidden, to then accumulate it all and 'spit it out, all at once'.
- Goal manifestation needs to be as realistic as possible, and they should remind themselves not to be too critical on oneself.
- How do you see the world, as perception becomes a powerful tool to live the moment. Their focus is on the place and people where they feel accepted. Family and friends become the focus as world.
- Trial: not to exclude themselves from the group, or hide behind excuses.

Knowing that the outcome of their studies is to help others, will make them want to study and be responsible.

Fifth CG
- They become freaks, and geeks, young perfectionists, with a need to be in the spot light, but have to work double to achieve that because of their innate fear and lack of self confidence.
- They want to look cool, but it is all a facade just to be accepted.
- They think know better and argue to be right.
- They don't let you in their inner world, disappearing often. Being fiscally next to you, yet so far away.
- Deep within they are very envies of others, and separate themselves, feeling different.
- As parents, they may blame you for their failures, and become resentful towards you. Please don't think it's you.

- Later in life when they stop focusing on others most of them become later on the confused professor, the scientist.
- To those who wish to know:
- People on the earth plane can only hold from the second to the fifth chakra as gift. Only a handful are blessed with the sixth as a gifted connection.

We are incredibly fortunate in one way and feel lost in another way. We have the four groups on one planet. Four categories of people who are completely and totally opposite from each other. Some moments it gives you new perspectives, but most of the time it confuses. Because we can only feel one part of what they find essential. For example; a number 5 is "all head and calculated actions based upon facts and reason", while a number three is all enthusiastic impulsive creative outpours.

Quite something this planet….different races, which even today still brings division among many. Then there are the high and low society, and now that we are going into cellular level, we see there are also 4 soul purpose groups. And then people speak of "world harmony"….

The communication bridge

to our inner self can only be three:

- clairvoyance, full intuition developed
- the pendulum, muscle testing, dealing with the immediate reality.
- living dreams, will power, goal orientation, feeling fulfilled

The higher conscious mind is not time-bound; means that when we worry too much we're activating the brain that is attached to the physical time space plain. Being in the moment for your conscious mind is living the 5 senses from the active or passive observer and being intuitive.

When you're not connected to the moment, you're activating the ego centered Tomas character. And we keep on carrying the preprogrammed old fashion tape recorder with us, wherever we go. A large part influenced by worldwide known commercials. A way to fit into society. Ever thought about why smoking, junk food and drinking problems are so tough to let go off? Perhaps it was shown on tv a few times a day and on top of that our parents had that habit, believing that smoking relaxes the nervous system, drinking made them overcome stress and forget about bills and payments. Repeated patterns are the hardest to let go off.

But in every Tomas resides 'om'...the omnipresence of God. The 'mas', meaning "more" in Spanish as in "not good enough" or "achieve more" attitudes.

The pendulum

The only inward communication that works for me and offers accurate results is the **pendulum**. I am aware that my intuition is just as powerful as the cellular communication, but I am still developing my third eye vision.

When I did my reiki initiation I was introduced to the pendulum system and was fascinated by this incredibly useful tool. Over the years I became an expert, but in the beginning it only worked when I wasn't tired, and most of the time in the morning. At first I played around with it like a toy and asked all sorts of insignificant questions. But then I became serious and respectful with it, after seeing I could rely on the answers. **One main point here: the pendulum itself does not answer our questions!** Our cellular system does, through the nervous system it reaches the finger and thumb holding it. This was the reason why when I was tired I could not connect to my cells.. My nervous system was altered, stress out, at a very low vibration. And for the pendulum to work we need to be peaceful and feeling serene.

First you establish yes or no. Asking very is simple questions, where you know the answer already. Holding the pendulum at about 15/20 cm from your hand, make a small circle wise movement and formulate your question, very relaxed. Get acquainted with it, the more you practice the more you start trusting it.

When you're dominating the pendulum with yes and no answers, then we can start with the 'scale from 1 to 12' questions. This is to help us achieve more accrued answers. So place the point of your pendulum on the center point, make your little circle and ask your question..

'on the scale from one to 12 how much % of …do I live of my soul's potential?

For instance if you want to know how you're doing on compassion these days, then ask 'On the scale of 1 to 12 how much % of compassion do I live of my soul's potential these days? Be specific, you can ask about last month, during your child hood, this week, any time,..

We can ask about sensibility, releasing, enthusiasm, empathy, intelligence, comprehension, vitality,.. and start asking very profound questions to understand better where we can grow, progress, become more enlightened, be healthier,..

Please do not be disappointed in the answers, work with it, listening to your thoughts around the topic and decide to be more aware and mature with it.

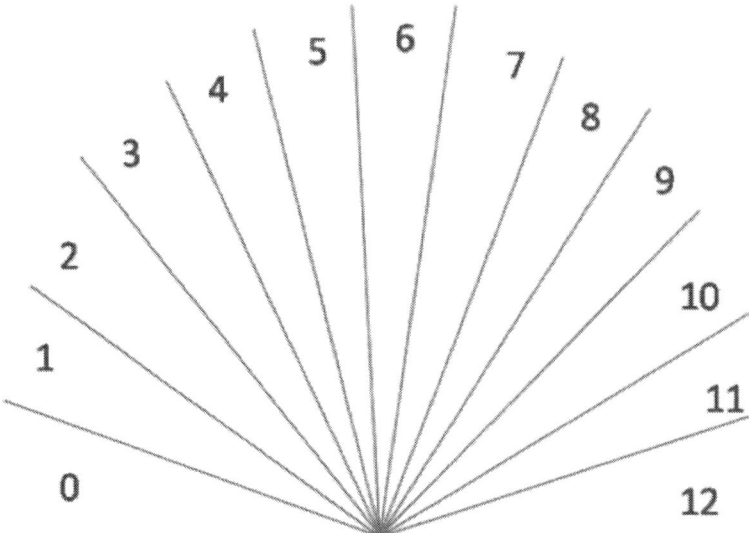

Chakra check up

Through the pendulum you'll understand how to connect to your 7 main chakras. Listen to what they communicate you. Each chakra in its own representation of divinity is an opportunity to live to its full potential. As I explained before already, your chakras have a vibration-expression, that can be seen like a soft transparent glow of warm colors around your body.

Compare your behavior, words, thoughts and feelings to the Universal Chakra Potential. Read and reread over and over the potential of each chakra and then envision the most successful precious expression of each one of them for you in your daily life.

If you're not able to work confident enough with the pendulum, then go with intuitive writing. Put your left hand on the chakra area, ask the question out loud and write the answers down without thinking about it.

Chakra 1
Is my 1st chakra in alignment with the universal light?   Yes or no

On the scale from 1 to 12, how much is this chakra working it its full potential?
How much on the scale from 1 to 12...
    ...do I have a feeling of belonging?
    ...do I act upon my dreams and heart desires?
    ...take firm steps, certain of what I want?
    ...do I apply passion for life?
    ...how much vitality am I circulating in my body?

Chakra 2

Is my 2nd chakra in alignment with the universal chakra? Yes or no
On the scale from 1 to 12, in general how much is this chakra working it its full potential?
How much on the scale from 1 to 12
...do I believe in abundance?
...am I grounded enough?
...do I have confidence in myself?
...do I see recognize my values and self-worth?
...is my gonads gland working properly?
...how am I doing on emotional balance?
...how much do I accept my physical body?

Chakra 3

Is my 3rd chakra in alignment with the universal chakra? Yes or no
On the scale from 1 to 12, in general how much is this chakra working it its full potential?
On the scale from 1 to 12....
    ...do I believe in creativity?
    ...is my inner child's joy and enthusiasm active?
    ... do I live in prosperity?
    ....do I feel inspired?
    ....am I motivated?
    ...do I see the soul and mission reflected in other people?

Chakra 4

Is my 4th chakra in alignment with the universal potential? Yes or no

On the scale from 1 to 12, in general how much is this chakra working it its full potential?
On the scale from 1 to 12...
> ...do I feel compassion for myself?
> ...do I have empathy for others?
> ...am I open to receiving gifts from others?
> ...can I be lighthearted?
> ...am I patient and tolerant?
> ...am I grateful?
> ...am I still influenced by others?
> ...do I feel victim of a situation?

Chakra 5

Is my 5th chakra in alignment with its universal potential? Yes or no?
On the scale from 1 to 12, in general how much is this chakra working it its full potential?
How much on the scale from 1 to 12...
> ...do I express my needs?
> ...do I detach?
> ...do I inwardly communicate to my system?
> ...am I seeing causes instead of coincidences?
> ...do I channel wise information?
> ...am I worried?
> ...do I still have judgmental behavior?

Chakra 6

Is my 6th chakra in alignment with its universal potential? Yes or no
On the scale from 1 to 12, in general how much is this chakra working it its full potential?
How much on the scale from 1 to 12...
> ... do I observe the totality of life?
> ...do I see the loving attentions on the actions of my loved ones?
> ...do I follow my intuition?
> ...do I enter in silent moments, reaching a calm state of mind?
> ...is the law of attraction activated in me?

Chakra 7

Is my 7th chakra in alignment with its universal potential? Yes or no
On the scale from 1 to 12, in general how much is this chakra working it its full potential?

- ♥ Highest potential in thoughts?
- ♥ Words?
- ♥ Actions?

Self-aid in chakra balancing

If you're capable of releasing energies through yawning or erupting, then you're well prepared to maintain your chakras connected to their source.

> *"The person healed has an obligation to then ask why, to meditate on God's will, and the extraordinary lengths to which God has gone to realize His will."*
> *— Stephen King, The Green Mile*

Procedure

- Breathing slowly three times.
- Feeling abundant saliva in your mouth.
- Totally still in your brain during those exhalations.
- Feel connected with your third eye to a peaceful space within.
- Then feel the light pass through your hands towards the chakra you're working with, making small circles with your hands at about ten centimeter distance.
- Affirm, "I now release the energies attached to this chakra which are blocking the universal power towards it."
- Keep on yawning or imputing till you feel the connection is clean.

- According to the chakra, read the evolved channeled affirmative prayers from the next pages, which you repeat maximum three times.
- Then feel the words settling in your system, repeating the above procedure.

When I use the word "God, the Universe" I mean it as the infinitely loving creative source and collective consciousness we can connect to and feel embraced and enriched in every way.

Saying a prayer is a powerful affirmation and a deep meditation. I am not religious, yet I worked with the compassionate power of the Christ or the Buddha often and respect, embrace and honor their selfless effort and devotion to the human race, and I am aware there is a power when we pray in their name.

I spend a lot of time in nature and retreat often in a monastery where I rest in the chapel, feeling peaceful and with a warm homecoming feeling.

These next prayer/ affirmations are extremely powerful and came channeled.

Don't forget to focus on the physical area you are working on as well.

First chakra

Dearest God,

I commit myself to take firm steps and honor as often as I can each space I occupy here on earth.
Guide me through the spiritual growth process while I learn to ground myself. The vital force raises from the base of my spine and I feel ignited with a powerful home coming-feeling and vitality.
I know I am embraced and guided by you during each step and this offers me a belonging feeling.
A healthy reproduction of stem cells occur in my system, as I know I depend upon the purity of the vital force existing in the air.
Respect for Mother Nature is part of my priority from now on. Thank you for holding my hand with every serene decision I take.
I feel honored to walk with you, on earth as in heaven.
Keep my loved ones safe as well.

I am grateful for this shift in me.

As it is

for I am a lightbeing

Second chakra

Dearest Father,

I recognize my values, virtues and know my self-worth.

From today on I shall no longer allow for emotional imbalances to affect my daily life and the lives of those who are dear to me.

The virtues offered by you enhance my life with genuine power.
True balance and harmony with nature and with all those I touch is my birth right and I shall respect it wisely.

Each time I breathe consciously in this peaceful way, I acknowledge and feel your sacred presence.

Each day I feel comprehend more who I am and feel more grounded… the duality existing on the earth plane no longer affects me.

I am truly grateful.

As it is

for I am a lightbeing

Third chakra

Majestic Life-force,

With each new morning show me how to feel more motivated and enthusiastic to be all I can be. My inner child expresses itself through me as often as you guide me to do so. The more I can connect to living my mission here on earth, the more prosperity is offered as opportunity.
I shall face each challenge presenting itself in front of me with courage and not make it larger than it is. Creativity is my key to being integrate and successful in my mission.
I shall shine my golden light igniting others with motivation and inspiration through my example.
I keep a healthy body weight, since I do a perfect digestion of every food intake, words spoken and thoughts so my system doesn't have to convert it in layers upon my body.

All is well with my inner being and each day I learn to mature in my experiences, yet never forget to apply the respected passion and spirited energy.

Eternally grateful for your warmth upon me.

As it is

for I am a lightbeing

Fourth chakra

Dearest God,

I am aware that life in society is challenging to say the least, and sometimes I take faith, hope and self-love as the last resource. Offer me examples of compassion along my path of life so I can expand my heart towards myself and in empathy to those who are worthy of entering it.

Being grateful and lighthearted in the moment in truly the highest form of living, since the past is already gone and the future is still to be manifested. And only when we are grateful and walk with a light heart can we activate the law of attraction and obtain quality life for ourselves and our loved ones

I shall be loyal and true to my sentiments from now on.

A warm green glow emanates from all my actions.
Thank you.

As it is

for I am a lightbeing

Fifth chakra

Dearest omnipresent source of life,

I choose to work upon my expression and communication capacity. Guide me so I speak, outwardly, wise words and supportive encouragements to those I love.
And inwardly, communicate with my inner innate intelligence imprinted upon my DNA and stem cells.
I am prepared to respect my emotional reactions, let go all drama and trauma and open my shoulders, walk straight and look people in the eye.
Allow me to shine a calm tone of blue, so it can be perceived as peaceful by those I come in touch with.

A million thanks for your presence in my own life, and in the life of my loved ones.

As it is

for I am a lightbeing

Sixth chakra

Dear Father,

I became aware that all judgmental behavior is only a waste of time, effort and energy. Help me to remain focused on seeing the totality, being the observer and witness without judging or blaming.

I choose to follow the inner guidance leading me to a more meaningful and significant experiences. Guide me to become a symbol of contemplation and have the warmhearted Christ Consciousness activated.

Allow this deep indigo blue to be activated within me so I can feel to be trustworthy, consistent with my priorities set in the right direction.

And through this effort I am aware that I shall be able to have my mind at ease, peace when I need it the most and serenity in my radiance.

With lots of love I thank you.

As it is

for I am a lightbeing

Seventh chakra

Dear creator of all there is,

I decide to honor my soul and spirit in as many of the words I speak, deeds I act upon and thoughts that move through my brain. I invite you to allow the higher purpose to happen through me as a pure channel of blessings to those who decide to bathe in this sacred light.
I shall henceforth stand my ground, believe in myself, recognize my cooperation here on the earth plane and allow only that light of my soul and spirit to be my reason
I shall allow my heart to celebrate this inner connection in gratefulness and righteousness. I believe now in integrity, the unification and respect of my physical, emotional, mental and above all spiritual body.

Kindly guide my loved ones to respect their higher self as well.

I am your grateful and devotional channel.

As it is

for I am a lightbeing

The silver cord between the red and green line

Important general questions to comprehend how much we are on the green or red line, and how to move up from one to the other.
Check with the pendulum from 1/12. If you're not very confident enough yet with the pendulum, you could try to connect to your intuition. But trust me, most of the time the stem cells (pendulum) have a "better answer" than the one we hold as a vision about ourselves.
The silver cord moves spiral-wise, up or down.

In order to move **spiral up**…

- "Pure intent" and comprehension is our first step.
- Open your heart, more compassion; more connection to others. Become more grateful, humbly grateful, to be able to enjoy basic life, basic needs, and be so grateful it hurts.
- Reach into the Akasic Records and remember….
  Passed lives are no longer "past"; past lives can be tapped in like an energy-field. The attributes you need to make your dreams happen during lifetimes you have earned your stripes.
- Remove drama.
- Stop being dependent how other react or treat you. So confident you become dependent only on God.
- Use the power of Intuitive thought; a map of which decisions to take, see your potential clearly.
- Become enthusiastic again, accept surprises, say "thank you" instead of "no thank you".
- Feel satisfied, content, fulfilled.

- Using the 9th layer of the DNA. Join the three-dimensional parts of the immune system and create a healthy body.
- Look past the face in the mirror, and see God reflected in your eyes.

Which mode am I on?

Achievers in life, truly successful people are not afraid of the truth as it is; rather it sounds positive or tough to handle.
We know we'll evolve and mature through any situation we're in. Our vision is under CAUSE, not coincidence, and since life will never be without challenges, obviously we'll also have our "time where we are down" ...and we'll need to make our way back up, out of the dark space, before it turns into quicksand.

The tree stages

1. The ALIVENESS MODE: The green line: fulfilled, peaceful, powerful, Alpha empowered.
    1a. highlight moments.
    1b. satisfaction, gratefulness, pride, contentment,..

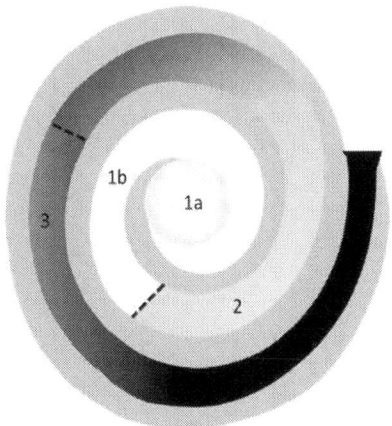

2. The COMFORT MODE survival mode: reserve energy mode, edgy, irritated, short lasting diseases, living on the edge

3. The LOST destructive mode: no hope left, fear of the next day, lost, developing painful chronic diseases.

I've witnessed and lived it firsthand several times!

In my book, Our Journey into Mastery you can read how I healed myself of thyroid cancer but the doctors didn't believe me till they saw the proof upon the removed organ,... so they still operated on me.

On the third day that I was home after the surgery, I was in shock by something I was witnessing!! Such an unjust situation!

In order to explain this, I need to go one year back, where this story started.

I had just finished building a wooden cabin on the terrace of the fourth-floor where I lived. So every morning I was enjoying breakfast outside, looking at the light penetrating my treasured cabin, feeling the breeze in the pine tree touching me and I started noticing a gentleman who, daily, and at the same time, passed on the street; he had to hold on to every street corner and catch his breath before he could continue.

Then he would sit on a bench at the corner of the street; read a book, placing his pocket radio next to him. I saw with a smile of appreciation that he was well shaved and impeccably dressed each and every single day. This went on for about seven months—same routine. I am never the least curious about my neighbors; don't ever interfere or invade their privacy. Yet I was intrigued by that gentleman. I truly admired him and looked forward to seeing him, and each time he was later than usual, I had been worried. He became part of my morning ritual. He had never looked up and was unaware of who I was.

Behind the bench he sat on, there was an old fort where the homeless guys used to gather and hang out in the afternoon and evening hours. But then, one day, on my way to the store, I saw one of the homeless guys sitting on the bench next to the gentleman. I had a bad taste in my mouth yet decided not to judge the guy; perhaps his only intention was just to enjoy the radio; no harm done there.

The next day, he was there again. Gradually more homeless people gathered on the bench in the morning. One month later, I saw the gentleman sitting among the drunks closer to the fort, still nicely shaved, still reading his book, still listening to the radio. I saw how he gave them money to buy their liquor.

A few months later, while I was about to have my surgery, he passed in the morning without shaving, without ironing his shirt, without radio or his book, and went to sit and drink wine and beer with the guys, a group that in that moment had become about 12 of them. My heart was in such pain, and I was furious but since I was in my own "tough spot" with having to be operated, I didn't to interfere.

Until that day; a few days after my operation, I was resting on my bed in my cabin with the windows open and I suddenly felt a pain in my heart, so I looked at the street and indeed, there I saw the gentleman lying on the ground! My own pain in my throat was forgotten as I screamed in shock! And in tears and explosive anger I walked down the stairs to help him as fast as I could move. It was raining and he must have slipped on the steps; he had blood on his temple and those guys were laughing and drinking. I picked him up as well as I could and caressed his face saying he would be all right. When I saw somebody pass on the street on a bike I asked the person to call an ambulance. When the ambulance arrived the police accompanied them and they thought it was just one of the drunks who had slipped due to too much alcohol, but I told them how he had been a very decent man just a couple of months before.

When I saw he was in good hands I realized I was exhausted and needed to rest again.

Right before leaving, I turned around and looked those drunken guys in the eyes; and trying to control my fury, I asked them if those few bottles of alcohol they got out of this man's wallet were really worth destroying his balanced and decent life.

It seemed they gotten more out of him than just that because when the police asked him where his home was, he told them that had lost his house to be able to pay for all the drugs and alcohol.

Vultures!

His sister covered for him, offering him her home from then on after he came out of the hospital.

I never saw him again, but I heard he recovered and recuperated his former personality.

1. Aliveness mode

Being on aliveness mode would mean to be in the moment with the silver cord towards our higher self-activated.
1a and b:
Highlight moments have a roller coaster effect. Moments where a deep joy, an embracive peace, a really happy feeling occurs, perhaps during a celebration, the falling in love or when a festivity takes place. As you can see this is where 1b comes in. Since the highlight doesn't hold any challenge; anybody can enjoy it; it is right after those moments where the opportunity for growth starts. How much can we allow ourselves to feel satisfied, grateful, be present, enthusiastic, open, free,.. Allowing the warmth of the highlight moment to settle in, to touch every corner of our being.
Key INVITATIONS are
- SATISFACTION
- GRATEFULNESS
- APPRICIATION appreciation

The aliveness mode can reach a long way. It can also be when we have a great idea, then while making it into a reality we might face challenges, falling and getting up included. During these courageous times we remain upon the aliveness area, since we are still connected to the life force, living purposefully.

With these question you can see how close you are exactly to your true being.
In the center of the spiral the person is connected to the Source of existence, plugged in if you want to see it this way.
You could take the pendulum or work with intuitive writing...
1 to 12
- How much time did I spend in alpha brainwaves the past week?
- How much time did I spend in theta brainwaves the past month?

These days....
- How often do I feel vital, energetic, not sick?

- How often am I inspired to be creative, and act upon it?
- How satisfied am I over my achievements?
- How compassionate and grateful am I?
- How often do I walk light on the street smiling at unknown people, even saying funny remarks.
- How often do I allow myself to just enjoy nature sounds, without added thoughts?
- Am I doing enough physical stretching and workout?
- Can I help my body to be healthier?
- How often do I listen do my intuitions?
- How often do I achieve set goals, manifests dreams, listens to my heart desires and acts upon them?
- How often do I help friends to reach their goals as well?
- How often am I authentic, innovative in creativity?
- How often am I unattached to the outcome, enjoying the action itself?
- Am I taking in enough nutritional foods to keep my stem cells healthy? From 1 to 12?
- From 1 to 12 how often do I imprint loving messages upon the water I take in?

2. Survival mode

A person who lived a painful or unjust experience may become defensive, protective or 'a loner'. What is called 'effectivity, getting things done' gradually becomes 'obsessive behavior'. Once in a while he experiences a peaceful or enthusiastic moment, then misses it so much he gets depressed. Starts resenting people close to him, responding harsh words, pretending he doesn't care. As a result suffers colds, headaches, depression, nervous and blood diseases.

In the stillness of his conscience he knows the truth and there are only two ways: stay ignorant, continue and get totally astray, lost in alcohol, drugs or workaholic addictions, or back to aliveness mode, grab the bull by the horses! Reality check up...

The questions one can ask to see how serious or deep did we're get in, are:

These days, 1 out of 12...

- How often am I disconnected from the cosmic energy?
- How often am I on reserve energy?
- How often am I disappointed in life?
- How often do I acknowledge my blessings?
- How often do I take selfish decisions, ignoring the need of his friends or family?
- How often do I get annoyed when someone close makes a mistake?
- Blames them for his mal-fortune or stress.
- Several chacras close due to the lack of energy flow in the etheric body, there is a lack of 'believe, communication or connection to God'
- How often do I feel that when someone does something nice, I thinks about how now I am obligated to give the person something in return, instead of feeling grateful for the gift offered.
- How often do I repeat negative events in my head, makes them bigger than they are?
- How often do I new objects, without truly needing it, just to feel 'good'?
- Am I becoming a perfectionist, focussing on mistakes?
- How often do I say 'I can't...'
- Have I lost inspiration?
- How often am I still justifying my actions to others?
- How often do I occupy myself constantly with burdens and work, finding excuses not to take a walk in nature, or breathe pure air in.
- How often do I have the feeling that an outside person controls my inner being?
- How often do I miss my old friends, but don't approach no one.
- How often do I perform one kind act, wanting to cover a few months of ignorance, and seek to be applauded for it.

- How often do I feel a heaviness in every step.
- How often do I feel the street has 'enemies'
- How often do I have problems getting up in the morning.
- How often do I feel moody.
- How often do am I surprised to I hear my own laughter.
- Is bothered by anything unexpected, like a person crossing, a door closing with noise, irritated.
- How often do I see the intention of someone's action, instead of how it feels like to me?
- How often do I need to force myself to be professional, kind, helpful to costumers.
- How often do I feel I 'must do things' instead of wanting to do things?
- One to twelve, how deep am I in this survival mode?

3. Destructive mode:
unconscious "inner death wish" mode

- Do I have a reason to get up in the morning?
- How often do I feel in the depth of despair?
- How often am I being a burden to others, playing a victimhood-game?
- How often am I in beta brain waves, no satisfied feeling, not offering myself a moment of relaxation?
- How often am I responding or reacting aggressively?
- How often do I enjoy the moment?
- How much is my the first chakra reacting upon my behavior?
- How much am I influencing so physical pain, serious illness settle in my system?
- How afraid am I going to bed, assuming the next day won't be better.
- How lonely do I feel, not understood?
- How often do I neglect my stem cells in nutrition?
- How often do I have a bulldog attitude?
- How often do I put up a mask in society, not showing who I truly am?

More secrets revealed on the how to get back

Use your intellectual capacity, raising it to a higher consciousness level

- Take the decision! I want out.
- Know you had go through it in order to evolve.
- When the old habit wants to repeat itself take control saying the words 'Now I know better'
- Motivation, start a creative project.
- Be humble, apologize to those you have done injustice.
- Enjoy your favorite soap, ask someone to wash your hair peacefully
- Focus on what you do have as blessings
- Relax during a Swedish massage
- Project inner visions where you will be more successful and loving in the near future
- Take firm steps on the street, open up your lower back and shoulders
- Listen to a friend who needs genuine help
- Ride a bike enjoying nature
- Repeat 'I am one with God', feeling more saliva in your mouth.
- Connected to the Theta brainwaves, "I am a channel of blessings to all those I touch in every way" keeping the channeling active.
- Drink lots of water, conscious, imprinting one moment of 'love' as you swallow it.
- Neem tea or St Jon's wort, as a nerve relaxation works wonders.

Part 2

Mastery

I finally realize…
I don't see the world through my eyes, I perceive the essence of nature and each person through the still conservative intelligence deep within in my breath.

"I
open
up
to
live
the
maximum
potential
within
this
opportunity."

We should aim to bring each event we undertake to its own center of existence.
Once we bring FULL CAPACITY of pure intent into the moment, it will be in synchronicity with the "source" and automatically it will find a flow to become a manifestation, despite of all the apparent obstacles it may encounter. But remember, only to its full potential can it become its maximum capacity of expression!

Full potential demands from us to be fully present, no distractions, no diversions,…
Confident, brave, encouraged, enthusiastic enough to make it happen. Then you give "the law of manifestation" time to line the occurrences up, so it can become a realization.
Other people may not share your interest, so as simple or insignificant it may seem to one, to another one it will seem important enough to make it the center of attention.

Don't do anything halfway, it is only an investment that asks for failure and waste of time and probably money.
A few of our projects
- Personal good living, health, friendships, hobbies
- Personal professional success
- Loving close relationships
- Expansion of intelligence

Each one of these expressions asks for full alignment with the source. One moment at the time, equally divided.

In the movie The Gods of Egypt Ra teaches his grandson Horus a lesson. Ra had given him two eyes to be able to transform him and rule in power. When Horus' envious uncle steals those eyes, Horus feels lost and acts like a poor victim.
After some time, when a warrior recuperates one of the eyes for him, Horus asks help from Ra to get his transformation power back.
The powerful Ra acts astonished when he approaches him, "You Horus have been lazy too long. Every God's life is a journey. You must earn it. When you stride from your path you grow weak son!"

Living for a higher purpose

The line that unites both fill us with
- Divinity
- Grace
- Blissfulness
- Immeasurable Love
- Peace
- Balance
- Lightheartedness
- Grateful
- Belonging feeling

Our Soul and Spirit perfect harmony

Our Higher Self is composed of Soul and Spirit as one Light, with two different essences, expressive and manifesting powers and attributes. When we pray or inwardly communicate it feels good to know the base of who we pray to.

Causal Encounters

I had started to observe patterns in our daily encounters and a friend told me about how we meet people for a reason, a season, or a lifetime. And it's so true. I like to see the universe operating as though it's one big puzzle, shifting and molding the pieces so constantly it all fits in. Our needs are met, and we feel grateful for the "right time, right moment" we were there. Carpe diem—seize the moment to the fullest—so we don't have to live in the "what if" shadow of the encounter, may it be reason, season, or a soul union time on earth.
Offer from our hearts without desiring something in return
from the same person.
Each person crosses our path for a certain time or experience. The sooner we see the category the person falls under, the sooner we can capture the message hidden in the encounter. I offer you my interpretation of encounters along our path of life.

A wish, a reason

When you utter the phrase "I would love to," the universe hears you and organizes the encounter needed for you to live that wish. Sometimes, it is through a song or a scene in a movie or through meeting a person who makes you realize your special wish. Or opposite, somebody has a wish and you're the one to aid in making it happen. Writers, cashiers, small town shops, movie producers, actors, singers, nurses, and/or doctors appear in people's lives for a reason, sometimes to alleviate the moment or to bring a smile to our face. You may say, "Cashiers? All they do is pass our groceries and receive our money." Let me tell you. Years ago, one Christmas evening, I was writing all day, and as the evening approached, Indy was tired and went to bed at 7 p.m., so I knew it would be another solitary Christmas. I went for a walk toward the shop to buy myself a little gift (chocolate) to accompany me during that special family night. I saw all the couples preparing themselves for the event. When I reached the cashier, I was struggling not to feel lonely. She had her head bent and one by one passed the groceries. Then it was my turn, and I passed my chocolate on to her. She smiled when she saw that was all I had and said, "I have also had moments like this." We looked each other in the eyes, and I touched her hand, saying warmly, "Merry Christmas."

That encounter changed the course of my evening and per-haps of my life. So, yes, cashiers can make a difference in people's lives. As a yoga instructor, each person in my class is "passing by," and I learned to offer as much as I humanly can, put my judgments aside, and tune into their DNA and soul level so in the short amount of time of one hour, they get as close to themselves as possible. And most of the time, I am the fortunate one. I have a meditation exercise where I plant an imaginative seed every day, and often I ask love as a reality to be manifested, and then these warmhearted, open guests appear in my class and love flows from them. Like butterflies, they caress my life.

A Season

People who spend some time with us usually teach us something we've always wished to learn—a skill, value, or virtue. They are people who awaken a profound sense of gratitude each time we think of them even though it may have been hard sometimes. Something ungoverned by both of us happens, and they move out of our life as silent as them came in.

Some of these life lessons need several teachers until we can learn them or until we can overcome our ego or fear to accept them. One person teaching us may not be enough. And we've all heard people say, "Strange, my friend told me the same thing last year." The message keeps on appearing with people who appear for a season, people who work upon the same level of vibration.

It's like a lifetime friend but hidden in different bodies.

Bringing in what we categorize negative or positive experiences, the message is always filled with love. Our soul wants us to learn the skill, add the value, and accept the virtue. We'll expand in light as soon as we see the cause of the repetitive encounters because that's when we usually start paying attention, after we've heard or seen something three times. Then those particular seasonal encounters can stop.

Many men or women keep on attracting the same kind of abusive partner, who spend a few seasons with them and then move on, until they learn to work on self-confidence and appreciate and respect themselves so the next person coming along can be of a higher, sweeter vibration level. Seasonal encounters who treated us unjustly are people we should say "thank you" to and wish them the best so we can detach ourselves and work upon our own space with the lesson learned and the loving moments settled.

One person entered my life when I was in my early twenties. I was in an advanced dance group, and we were practicing a dance act for the opening of several sports events and shows. And one week before our first performance, my dear friend, who was a known model in my country, had an accident. She lived in the city close to me and picked me up so we could go together to the rehearsal four times a week for twelve weeks already. The conversations in the car had always been very profound, and we had a lot of fun in the class because the other dancers were professional dancers, and we were the only clumsy followers. Of course, after so many weeks, we practiced extra at home, so we also managed to be at the level of the "professionals." She was such a wonderful person inside the body of a top model. She taught me with her presence in my life that you need to enjoy the person you are to the maximum at the age and stage you're at. And being a top model doesn't mean being superior; she was sharing and warmhearted, and before knowing her, I used to judge the pretty girls.

What happened to her? She had a gas leak. She came home after our class, and by opening the door, the apartment exploded. Twenty-five weeks of hospital belaying, unrecognizable, total loss of her skin, no longer a top model, no longer beautiful in her appearance, and tortured with a deep trauma that would also change her emotional and mental state. She didn't want to see anyone who knew her from before the accident when she was recuperated, me included. After what happened with her, I never went back to the dance group. Neither did I get a chance to hug her.

I embrace my one-season friend now and feel fortunate to have enjoyed her beautiful spirit. I hope she has somehow restored her personality and found strength to live her life purpose as the warmhearted person she rooted inside of her.

A soul family union on earth

True loved ones who remain faithful in their love during the time they are by your side, a day, a year or a few decades. And even though we have the feeling they can be counted on one hand, when we come to think of it, actually they are much more send to us during one lifetime.

They are the ones who pull us through our biggest trials. They will rip the mask from our faces and put a mirror in front of us, challenging us to see the false attitudes we hide from the outside world.. They'll argue with us and say, "You don't have to believe me, but please see for yourself."

Those are the people who wait patiently until you awaken and are ready to live up to your potential. They will stand by you, whether you kick them, push them away, or love them. Their purpose is to follow their intuition and to know you are meant to be together now or in the near future no matter what the wind brings. Only death can separate you until you decide to live a next existence/life together. I recognize my grandfather in my daughter, the same strength and valor, the same silent presence. I believe that with those soul family unions, we also have a bond beyond time and space, and we work through synchronistic renewal of energy with each other.

Have you noticed that when a friend/family member hurt you somehow, after some time, you are able to just forget about the incident and you realize that love had never abandoned either of you?

I believe that "soul family" are the people we just can't do without, may it be in lifetime, decade, or shorter-encounter-span people. It's a sacred union that demands to be honored and embraced. When there is a gap created between them and you, don't you feel lost somehow, thinking about it too often?

Story
He Waited for Her Faithfully

All though all my sessions are kept in secret and I never reveal them, I want to share this story of a couple I met years ago right after my thyroid-removal surgery.

When I restored the hormonal balance about a month after the operation, I reinitiated to offer some massages on the beach during weekends. That's where I found this profound lesson on soul family encounters.

For about two years, during the summer, I had been giving massages on the beach and had several regular customers. When I was recovering, taking a walk along the coast, I met one of them, Dolores. Since she saw I was doing okay, she asked me if I could offer her a massage. Her eyes told me she was in need. Dolores was a sweet, balanced lady, and my massages to her never touched my own energy force. With that in mind, I loved the idea of helping her.

In those days, I still hadn't learned to manage fully the fact that as therapist, or people who touch others, we work with the divine energy, not with our own energy. It is through us, not from us. The most powerful sentence is, "I am a channel of blessings to all those I touch in every way, now, today, always. I am one with God."

(In my workshops, I go very profound on this topic because I find it important that people don't end up drained after a day on the job, or getting home exhausted without being able to enjoy quality time with their family and friends.)

The problem and fortune was that it was summer and the beach lovers saw me giving the massages and decided to enjoy the same privilege, so after a few days, I found myself giving three to five thirty-five minute massages a day. On one of those days, a gentleman approached me when I had just started to initiate a new session. He wanted to say something, but I put my hand up, indicating to wait until I finish.

I never speak or divide my attention from the person I work on. He sat down, and I closed my eyes, focusing. When I came behind the lady to start her head massage, I saw he was still sitting there, waiting, so I signaled with my hand ten more minutes. He nodded yet didn't move. He looked peacefully out over the sea. I guessed he was sixty-five years of age, and with his serene and tender aspect, he touched my heart profoundly. I finished the massage and embraced the lady, and as she walked back to her beach chair to continue in this dreamlike state, the gentleman approached me. He asked for a massage for his wife. I admired his patience even more now and added the silent thought, "I hope that, one day, I'll meet the man who'll offer me this kind of respectful treatment." I was exhausted actually, but I couldn't send him back, denying his petition. So I asked if his wife was on the beach, which was answered as affirmative, and if I would have to get to her, if in case she was incapable of getting to the place where I was working. No, he would get her. I asked to give me ten minutes to be able to eat an apple first, promising myself that, that would be it for today—five in a row. I did my cleansing ritual, washing my hands and feet in the sea, and my throat got stuck suddenly when I heard that voice behind me saying, "Can we finally begin please? I only have two more weeks of holiday left." I thought, "Two deep breaths, Sandra. You can deal with her energy. It's just another wounded kitty." She gave me her towel, so I opened it and put it on my table. Her husband came with a small towel and cleaned her feet with gentle caressing strokes as soon as she laid down, then she told him to take her watch off so she doesn't lose it, looking at me. After a quick exchange of looks between her husband and myself, he walked away with the hand towel and the precious watch. This lady handicapped? Nope. Spoiled, definitely. On the tip of my tongue, I had, "Gosh, lady, you are so lucky with your husband," but she spoke first, saying, "My husband doesn't love me. He gives me headaches. Here is the money. I'll need several massages from you because of him!" I stood nailed to the ground. My stomach twisted, and I was about to throw her off my table. Reminding myself not to judge, to be professional, I took another deep breath and asked her to be still so I could concentrate on the energy flow. Before I could silence my brain, I thought about the amount of women who would give their life just to be loved for one week the way that man loved his wife. How was it possible that she didn't recognize his dedication to her? Then I did my utmost best to stop that hamster in my head from eating my energy and focused on divine love. Every massage stroke, I accumulated a little more until after half an hour, I could finally touch her the same way I touched Dolores, with profound sincere gentleness and an empty neutral brain, the combination I call tantric touch. Normally, it takes me five breaths to tune into this space. That time, it took me almost the entire massage. I felt every blockage in her being, where she resisted, where she accumulated hatred, denial. A body filled with knots, charged with heavy emotional rejections. I didn't stop yawning. (Yawning is my way to release their excessive tension or stress through my body instead of storing it.) When we were done, she wanted to come down from the table, and the first words she said were, "I am too fat. Don't know if I can get down." My body was empty, exhausted by then, and all I really wanted was to go home, lay down, and be in my own space. But I couldn't leave her in the hole she had made for herself, so I placed my finger against my mouth, saying, "Shhh! On this table, we never say anything negative about one's self or those we love. This space is to learn to appreciate and accept oneself, not to destroy oneself." It was clear she wasn't used being told to do or not to do something because she looked insecure suddenly.

Back then, I still didn't give the astral meditations after the massage, but I made her sit up and put her back against my chest and made her release the remaining tension from her neck and shoulders, bending forward, dropping her head, then back against my chest, and resting her head in my shoulder opening. And slowly, her defensive system melted. I rocked her like a baby and held her at my chest. The last time she repeated the exercise, I told her, "Feel how this relaxed state embraces your difficult moments and how, right now, as you bring your body firm and straight again, you can open your eyes and recognize your own value. You can clearly see the precious woman you are."

Yes, I was exhausted, but I had done the right thing.

She asked for an appointment in a few days and offered me some more money in my hand, which I normally reject, but with her, I accepted it. I knew how hard it was for her to give from the heart.

Her husband was waiting for her already to help her down.

On my way back, I held the extra tip she had given me in my hand, smiling. I knew her process wasn't over; we just started it. Reaching home, my menstruation started heavy. The next day, I was at the beach to practice tai chi, and no one would think of interrupting somebody profoundly in meditative state. The 108 movements take about half an hour of concentration, and I truly enjoyed that sacred practice. Halfway into my practice, my dear new friend tapped on my shoulder and told me that she needed a massage the same day. I asked her to step aside and let me continue first then I would talk to her. I focused again, finished, and told her that I couldn't give her a massage that day 'cause while having my menstruation period, I didn't have enough reserve energy to deal with her rejection and defensive energy field. I gave her some positive affirmations to work with so our next massage, planned in a few days, would be effective.

The day after that next massage, I met her on the beach, and she told me she had stopped insulting herself. Her father used to tell her she was ugly and fat, and she repeated those words daily in the mirror. Her husband, standing next to her, nodded, saying, "I tell her daily how beautiful she is, but she never believes me. At least she listens to you." She said proudly, "Look, Sandra. Today, I can put a bathing suit on and walk the beach feeling good without thinking about what people would think of me. You did a miracle upon me." She permitted it to happen and worked hard toward it.

We continued working together a few times more, and twelve days later than the day I met her, I saw a different woman. Walking toward her chair, I was about to salute them when I saw her husband coming out of the sea. There was a strong wind that day, and he was shivering. She surprised me by getting up with a large towel in her hand, walking toward him, embracing him with the towel, and, rubbing him dry, kissing him. He touched her face tenderly with tears in his eyes. I backed up and walked to the other side of the beach, drying the tears in my own eyes. A little later, I joined them to say good-bye, and after she embraced me, he whispered, "I married Maria forty years ago knowing she had this loving capacity in her, and thanks to your dedication and love, she finally let it rise to the surface. My faith and patience has been rewarded. I found my wife on this holiday."

When I reached my bike to leave, I could feel his look upon me, so I turned around, and my smile said, "Everything will be fine." His lips made a "thank you."

Light always prevails darkness, even if it lasted forty years.

Among soul family, it only takes a few days' time to open the door.

Through experience I realized that a healing process and journey within was incredibly insightful, uplifting and in the same time painful.

Yet, ignorance is NOT bliss. Having the courage to heal an inner wound is proof of dignified living. In moments where you yourself are going through it, be brave my new friend and face each phase of the process with your head up. Our guiding energy is with you along your journey.

A warm hearted scene from the touching movie The Spitfire Grill, directed and written by Lee David Zlotoff.

If a wound grows really deep, the healing of it can hurt almost as bad as what caused it.

12 layers of awareness levels

In direct connection with the collective consciousness.
Once we have gone through the purification and reside most of our time upon the green line, **then what?**
Then we apply to our own life that which we have obtained as a certainty; we enjoy life, and we teach others, mostly through example. We choose wisely, in synchronicity with our true potential.. we use the law of manifestation through focusing upon and acting upon that we feel is "right" for us. We live in the mastery level of life.

The more choices we make to respect and honor our level of awareness, the deeper we can penetrate in the Consciousness of Creation. We can tune into the Oneness Collective Consciousness, the natural flow of Love, through many portals, from which I offer a few in detail later. Once we have learned to tune into them, we can recall it and retrieve it from our memory. Once it is known and repeated a few times, it is stored and it can never be 'unknown' again. Here is my chart to how we as human beings have the ability to touch the Source

The Oneness Collective Consciousness IS Creation in LOVE

Conscious Choice allows us to select our thoughts, and accept only the productive, light, creative ones. Each day that passes we develop a more powerful intellect. Which is key to make choices and remain emotionally balanced.

Flow: Consequences of the decision to respect and honor Reality As It Is, allows us to flow automatically in the realms of intelligence, creativity, intuition. Gradually we become the observer, and thus tune into the higher Realms.

The 12 layers are divided in
- 9 layers in the Astral level.
- 3 layers in the Causal level.

Very dedicated, evolved people like the Buddha or The Christ are at the 11th level when they manifested themselves to the earth plane. We can only inspire to reach with lots of dedication to the 9th or 10th level.
How "far" we reach depends upon the light and evolvement of our soul.
We as humans can't reach into the causal planes with our awareness, when our soul is of the Astral planes.
The 9 layers of awareness in the astral realms, are our capacity of comprehending, living, acting upon, working upon and feeling the ESSENCE of the REALITY AS IT IS through our conscious mind. We're not judged, we're reminded of what's real, that's all. According to the level we live our daily life, we feel lighter or heavier.

Levels 1 to 12:

1: Lost in the consumption circle of 99 means spending earned money on stuff we will never be satisfied about, in company of people that uplift our ego, an ongoing struggle to reach 100, being absorbed by lesser quality habits and fast life, encountering many obstacles, occupied with the opinion and influences of others without feeling the connection to one's inner truth: 75% of the people reside in it competing and obsessed with each other instead of with a true meaning for life.

2: Duality, starting to believe something more exists, uncertainties rise, questions come up. In this state they start to acknowledge that a change is needed and fight hard against the upcoming doubts and fears. Old habits start dying a slow death, in persistence and knowing that we can forgive ourselves for the ignorant state we have been in. We go through the transformation period doing our best not to blame others for our past.
3: We are aware coincidences don't exist; everything has a cause, less judgmental behavior, blaming or doubting. Less side-tracking at this stage. We stop pointing at, looking at others for things that happen in our daily life. Coincidences no longer exist, we find a message in each encounter, for a short or long-time lived relationship or bond.

4: We know we have a soul, a purpose, are preparing ourselves to live it as a priority, in purposeful life, and are sending light to other people, through the power of intention and dedication. We have enthusiasm and a pure desire to find fulfillment.

5: Each day more, certainties are starting to settle, we feel we belong. We find ways to uplift our fellow man. Become compassionate in our connection to others. Gentleness is awakening in our touch and words.

6: We work upon our thoughts, reconstruct our though patterns, manifesting our basic realities and feel more inner peace and offer the enhancement in energy of our fellowman as a shared priority. We walk a straight path, no longer side track for long periods, and are honest and open about our interpretation of what we believe in. We stand up for our truth, and often stand out for it at this stage.

7: We are true to our power, no longer lingering into the lower energy vibration thoughts and emotional reactions. We learn to practice affection, unconditional love and comprehension with our loved ones. We are more receptive to the path they take, the process they live, and give them space, while we focus on ourselves. Sending light daily to the earth-plane and to our loved ones.

8: We live the infinite love as our guide, feeling the warmth in our heart, we learn to be in our sweet spot as self-love, connect to our astral body, and share with others in pure harmony, prosperity is at our grasp. Every single encounter becomes sacred by now. Our intuition is fully activated.

9: The old spiral is closed here with a whole ness healing. After a profound cleansing, that may be painful; a true home coming feeling appears, lasting long periods of time. We live for our soul's expansion. We remain in safety, knowing all is well. Rather that is with a partner in our daily life, or by ourselves, we truly feel embraced. Only a handful humans reach this level, it takes a lot of commitment to settle this height of consciousness in our DNA.
10: The power of manifestation is fully activated, our emotions are grounded, no longer influencing in the results in our daily life, so the intentions become our realities effortless. We live for God, in His name.

11: The compassion of the Christ is happening through us, we can observe, and choose to be or not be involved. We accept the flow of happiness and joy and welcome it in our daily life.

12: We touch the light of God, are One and can co create at any level, we can be, and with it live our mission.

ACTING upon the KNOWING

Do you know the feeling to be wondering, studying, preparing yourself, seeking, but it seems as though, no matter how hard you try, it keeps on being a dream without realization? I lived that feeling for about 14 years. Positive steps forward, set intentions, ..yet no real manifestation. Then suddenly it happened, it all started to go fast, high speed. What did I do, I wondered?

As you know, I had been writing about 20 diaries, sacred information channeled to me I was fascinated about, but I did not have the confidence to put it in a public writing, since I did not study literature and admired writers of books and screen players of movies far too much to consider myself one of them. I thought it was something out of my reach. So why did I have all that wisdom passed on to me? Then I had practiced martial arts half of my life and the chi gong movements gave such a sense of belonging in the moment, that I didn't understand how there could be people out there who lived with stress, when the solution was right under their noses. Food intake, the same thing, I had observed the reactions of my body and established a communication flow between my body and myself, and I could help so many. I had become a store house filled with Divine Knowledge, but to me it felt like a volcano about to erupt. And a few years ago I saw my mission reflected in the Cosmic Calendar, as serpent, order of wisdom, create open doors for people who seek. So I stopped fighting and accepted my gift and said:

'Yes, I DO! I am willing to live my mission and purpose as a priority, no matter what.'

This was not just a spoken phrase, this had been years of action, building up on a solid foundation, years of preparation, at first apparently going against the stream.

I stopped living the life of others; stopped adjusting according to the needs or rules of others. Others are those who have opinions about how it is all supposed to be.

As soon as you acknowledge this certainty: The law of attraction is activated at high speed.

Story

A few months out of the year, Palma de Mallorca has a "problem" I would call spectacular.

Hordes of birds fly in unison, perfect synchronicity between each one of them. They make forms in the sky, which provoke every person to enjoy the beauty of unity. The problem for the people from the island lies in the fact that those birds need a place to stay overnight, and the accommodation they tend to choose didn't suit them. Hundreds of birds enter the trees in the center of town and drop their rests on the cars and sidewalks.

They have tried everything to remove them. Gasses, shooting—name it, they tried. And when I overheard the conversation what they would do to them the next week, I was ashamed of the human race. I remembered my shaman friend with his bull. Domination of doubt and openness allow us to communicate to animals. And I stood on my terrace overlooking the city. I connected with my entire being to the collective consciousness of those birds. So much compassion ran through me. I wanted to help them before they become just another name in the history books.

And believe me or not, my daughter as my witness, I came through. I don't believe in coincidence anymore. Second revelation of the celestine prophecy, "There is a cause in everything."

When we pay full attention to something, it is meant to be our experience. I spoke to them, and they came. The evening set, and I saw them make their forms over the city a few kilometers away, and as I had been doing all day, I called them again, promising them a safe night in the pines in our street. I went inside because I had some food on the stove, and a few seconds later, I heard my daughter shouted my name with urgency. The colors of the sunset were blocked over my house. Hundreds of birds encircled it, and then they rested in the trees in my street for the first time. I sat there on the chair on my terrace, nurturing myself with the sound of their song and felt touched. Each bird had their own tone, yet together, they formed an orchestra and placed the most satisfying smile on my face I ever felt. They stayed the migration time they spent on the island close to me. With every sunset, they came home safe. At dawn, they started their symphony again, then as if someone pulled a switch, they moved out of the trees as one and started to draw forms in the sky. When you see only one, you would never give it a second glance, but when they are united, they are powerful, majestic, precious gifted birds. I was in love and felt loved.

Collective consciousness

How exactly do you create a universe around you?

When we, as individuals have a goal we start manifesting to help others, in its center, Universal Love is present in the form of a Radiant Light.

It may have reached us in a dream, a vision, or seen in somebody else's blissful expression when they are enjoying it and we got hypnotized by it. When curiosity entered our system, through free will we made it part of our life. In this process, each person started off as a student, until we dominated it and became experts in the field. As the years passed, we became more experienced, certain and efficient in it and obtained mastery. Most of us have forgotten how important our work actually is to others. And for some people a mission is something they've been doing for years, as a hobby, an interest, something we did off-work. But we were so focused on the 'making money job', that we did not realize that parallel, we were gaining experience in that which makes our heart beat in love, that which matters most, our soul mission.

Each individual has a different form of expressing the Universal Love. As nurse, dentist, instructor, cashier,..if our profession is felt from the heart it gives us purpose, an income and most importantly a sense of belonging. The more Light radiates from our work, the more people we reach, the more prosperous we become.

In mission fulfillment, we work with the Cosmic Energy, having unlimited resources as long as we stay aware of it. We know by now that when we can be in silent meditation for a few moments a day, we tune into the Astral Realms and we are ignited by Cosmic Energy, so we can continue to fulfill our mission, and have a lighthearted feeling.

This lighthearted feeling is the reflection of a Soul and Spirit activated in a person. When we take on the paper of Mastery, then the Collective Intelligence/ Consciousness expands through our loving intentions.

For example, in my classes I may touch 15 people a day, and on my website let's say 300/day and the loving words expressed are passed on, and on,.. this is how a network is created. Can you see the essence of Love in each one of our expressions? A nurse will have a different interpretation and perception than a school teacher when she passes her loving vibration on, yet the Home feeling we sense in our heart when we watch a scene of a movie, hear a sentence in a song, the caress of the nurse, it contains the same vibration, doesn't it. You see it is the same Universal Love, yet expressed in a million different ways here on earth?

Did you stop and think about all of this for a moment? Whatever our professional mission is, it is important to remember that it is our astral being, our inner guide who operates through us in the manifestation of our mission. On a moment to moment, daily basis. We need to keep an open view, and be still within, so the highest possible expression can manifested itself towards those we are in touch with. No anticipation, just go with the flow. Success is guaranteed, the more we learn to give room to our inner self.

So how to increase our income?

Project in a visualization how many people shall benefit from your teaching/work,.. And how they shall pass it on. Visualize a network of people in love with each other as a result of your effort and input.

Remember, our soul mission is related to being responsible while the purpose of our Spirit is a light hearted expression. Have fun and share joy in our daily life.

My daughter brought a story home from her class at the school, written by Paulo Coelho. "La margarita y el egoismo"

>-"I am a margarita in a field filled with margaritas" thought the flower. "In the middle of the others it's impossible to see my beauty".
>An angel heard her thought and answered:
>-"But you are so beautiful!"
>-"I want to be exceptional!"
>Not to hear more complaints, the angel moved her to a square in the city. Days later the mayor passed by the gardens with the intention of reforming the gardens. "There is nothing interesting here, plot the land and plant geraniums".
>-"Wait a minute" shouts the margarita 'When you do this, you'll kill me!"
>-"If there would be more of you, it would be a nice decoration" responded the mayor "but since I can't find other margaritas in these surroundings, you by yourself don't form a garden."
>And he pulled the flower out.

If you feel you have a special gift, please don't doubt your capacity, and don't get distracted by "competition". Just prepare yourself to your maximum capability. The power of your inner guide will make you be successful and be trustworthy in the eyes of those who seek. Keep your shoulders open and your head up when you announce your mission to the world. "Here I am. I am ready to share my gift."
Firm steps forward.

Each human being is drawn to another because the Soul seeks expansion in knowledge and Spirit seeks light.

These are the five general pillars Soul and Spirit want you to build upon:

joy

love

peace

harmony

fulfillment

BASIC NEEDS which every single person on the planet seeks to enjoy daily. People who don't get to feel this are easy targets to become out of balance, confused lost, lonely and ill.

You all appear in each other's lives to help one another expand..
The sooner you discover who you actually are related to society you can see the 'meaning' of your encounters, the more you become light hearted.
You know you're expanding your inner wisdom and light when you can smile often, when you can enjoy the moment. Soul and Spirit are seeking only one thing: for each person to be light hearted so you can live the reality, not just the physical visible proof of life.

A last wish

When I was only two months in Vallarta, a dear friend of mine from my yoga classes in Tepic called me to ask for help.

Her sister was suffering very much, and without questioning it, I took the six-hour round-trip bus twice a week to offer her assistance. Sometimes when I lose sight of the beauty of my heart, these precious events in my life renew my certainty that I am truly loving and being loved.

In order to comprehend this story well, I want to offer you this information first.

The activation of our first chakra has two major objectives—a rooted belonging feeling related to comfort in family, home, and job and having overall health and vitality. When I was explaining this to Juan Carlos, one of my costumers, he asked me, "Sandra, do you think it is weird that I can smell people who are about to die?" No, it is unusual that he is this sensitive, but it is not odd!

The reason why he smells people who are about to leave their physical body is because they close their first chakra. The life force doesn't renew itself in the body any longer. Stem cells stop regenerating themselves, and this reaction offers a particular smell. Each person who closes the first chakra has a life-threatening disease or the age to depart. My first question to the person when I detect this is, "Do you want to continue living, or is it truly time to rest?"

And if they chose to rest, I ask, "If you could choose one last event in your life before leaving this life, what would it be?"

In depressive attitudes, most people are not even aware that they have an underlying death wish because most probably, the "I can't anymore, I have enough…" thought patterns are stored in the subconscious mind. We want to forget the negative occurrences as soon as possible, yet our memory has absorbed the "I can't anymores" each time we pronounce them or felt them intensely. Note that it is extremely important to eliminate those statements from our vocabulary. Even though we may be accustomed to saying them without really meaning them, and five minutes later, the situation will calm down to such extent we're strong again to face reality and continue in a positive attitude. Remember that our body has stored them as valuable information pronounced. Law of attraction.

When the word got out in the small towns about my capacity to help people through these challenging times, the local people asked for my assistance. It required a lot of energy and love because most people I encountered in that situation were suffering from a disease and the family felt impotent and sad, and I did my best to create harmony in the painful departing situation.

I give the people who were about to depart the opportunity to validate their existence, look at all the values and virtues they had along their life, and recognize the difference they made on the earth. And in a deep meditation, they can embrace the light they are about to meet, comprehending they are safe. Serenity often invites the person to observe life and situations from above, and even an entire lifetime of depressions and fear can be released in one meditation when enough peace is felt as the center. I make sure the energy flows freely in the other six chakras, aiding them through the process of thought patterns and emotional blockages, which they may have accumulated along their lives, allowing them to be free of karma when they depart, accepting the messages. I don't really fully grasp the idea of several lifetimes lived and more to come, but I know the importance, in the first place, of being as free as possible of traumas and lost dreams and, in the second place, of living the true potential of our soul and spirit. A next lifetime would be initiated in health, prosperity, and love, and less grief and suffering would exist in the world.

In those last days, after unblocking the chakra flow, when a person decides through free will to send loving energy to people on earth; to be kind to the family members surrounding and supporting them; to express compassion and gratefulness to them; and to communicate with our physical body for having offered us a great life and, in sickness, through the pain, even finds lightheartedness; then there is true freedom, and the entire lifetime can be embraced with an happy ending. It seems like a lot of responsibility for a person weakening, but the truth is that I have seen it happen so often already that I know it is possible for every person to transcend the painful situation and make the most of the entire lifetime.

People in hospice centers or hospitals should open the flow of the six chakras. Make them aware of this opportunity.

Those who are about to leave and can accept it are extremely sensitive to the spirit world and can tune in easier than the rest of us in busy society. I would love to offer you here a standard meditation, but the truth is that each person is so different that it needs to be personal in the moment channeled meditation. What I can tell you is that they need a foot, head, and shoulder massage to relax themselves deeper, then start by guiding them through a beautiful visualization. I share with you here one of the meditations that appears often when it is a lady.

During the short massage, you ask her to relax her eyes and focus on how her breath is peaceful. Then while still caressing her hair, tell her to envision a flower field, many colors, warm sunlight, a gentle caressing breeze, and that she is wearing an elegant white knee-long dress moving with the breeze around her body. The path between the flowers is of soft forest ground, and she wears no shoes. Up ahead, a bright light awaits her patiently, and she moves toward it with firm, calm steps, enjoying her surroundings and her blissful grace in full. When she approaches the light, she feels such serenity and safety that she knows she is home. As soon as she's embraced by the light, she has a feeling of being so light she can fly and is lifted up in the air toward the most dazzling scenes she has ever imagined. And there she sees all her loved ones in the true light they are. And she sees and feels the precious true identity she is and has been along this life, right underneath the physical presence.

When it is a man, the meditation flows more in line of a puma, forest, speed, swiftness, pride, and, when penetrating the light, unity with the eagle soaring through the heights in freedom. I have seen very good results when I ask about his favorite sport or hobby, which he used to practice, and make him one with it again.

A few times a year, I offer workshops if hospice volunteers or nurses want to obtain mastery in life coaching and chakra balancing, aiding those who leave the earth plane and their dear family.

One of those precious people who left the planet was Emma. I shall share her story here. When I was aiding Emma, I was helping four people die peacefully that same week, but none of them touched me so deep as she did.

Emma was 75 percent paralyzed for many years and practically lived like a plant, having those who love her carry her everywhere and feeding her. Her sisters, who had joined my yoga class in Tepic, asked me to work with her. Before the stroke, Emma had been a kind, warm teacher and gave heart to everyone who came in touch with her. How can such a devoted person spend the last years of her life in such suffering? It seemed so unfair. Her sisters couldn't stand seeing her shrink away that way and asked me if I could bring more aliveness in her. The first time I saw her, I felt a very strong connection because of her big heart. Her eyes looked at me very gratefully when I massaged, relaxed her system, and nurtured every cell and atom with oxygen. I could sense it but saw it affirmed. She had closed her first chakra. As soon as I was certain, I took her sisters aside and asked them their opinion—opening the flow of energy again in her body or allowing the flame to die out. She couldn't speak anymore, so I couldn't really have a conversation about her true needs. She could move her left hand, though, and when I asked her something, she responded with a squeeze in my hand. She still wanted to "continue living," was her answer when I explained to her about the closed chakra. For her sisters? Small squeeze. Something she still wanted to do? Yes. I asked her sister about what Emma loved doing besides giving classes. Dance! I asked her, "Emma, quieres bailar?' and she closed her eyes. Then with a tear rolling down her cheek, she squeezed my hand firmly. "Yes." In her healing, I worked profoundly with the Christ vibration, knowing she had a strong belief in Jesus, the physical representation of such powerful, compassionate energy force. Every few days, I went to see her, and each time, the chakra closed again, and I kept on opening the vitality flow because her body could not provide healthy cells on its own any longer.

With the massages, her blood circulated well, and she became stronger, and I shall never forget her first smile after a long time of being able to use those muscles. And those hand-squeezing exchanges between us made us silent partners. Yet what lingers in my heart is the greatest gift someone can give another person. Share the more precious last moments of your life doing what you love the most. It took me eight sessions to restore her blood circulation and strength in her legs, feet, and hips, enough to be able to stand up with my help. You should know that I gave these therapies at their home and they have a dance studio for weddings and special events, so in the middle of the dance hall is where I worked upon her.

When I felt she was ready, I asked her sisters to bring Emma her favorite music, but since the songs were too quick, I chose a song sang by a nun who has the most beautiful voice, singing "nothing is impossible for you" in Spanish, "Nada Es Imposible Para Ti," in a mix with the type of music she used to dance to. First, I did the healing session, massaged her again, placed some constructive affirmations upon her system, and then we closed the curtains. Her sisters switched the golden light ball on, and when it started to turn, it lit the entire place with small stars. Emma, like a small child, looked fascinated by the lights moving around the ceiling and walls. Helping her get up from the lying position, I made her stand up on her own as much as she could. And then I waited for her in the middle of the dance floor, and she needed to take three steps to me. She did. I was so proud of her I thought I would burst. When the melody started with a perfect clear sound, I was the one shaking with so many emotions touching my heart. And with those powerful words as our guide, we moved very elegantly on one stone together, dancing. She did her best not to lose her balance or lean on me. Her entire existence was shown in her strength. Precious Emma. When I helped her to sit in her wheelchair, I asked her if she wanted me to work with her again, and she shook her head just a little, holding my hands firmly with a warm look in her eyes. I knew what that meant. When I got on the bus a little later, I couldn't tune into the spiritual benefit of leaving the earth plane with death. I was never going to see her again, and I allowed the tears to fall. I loved her so dearly, but I had to let her go.

She parted a few weeks later, with many people who knew her joyous character remembering her in their hearts. Emma honored me with the most precious baile I've danced and perhaps one of the most profound moments of my life. Her last wish fulfilled.

As you can see, I am a little bit too sensitive to help people and the families personally on a daily basis in hospitals. If you're a nurse, a doctor, or a hospice volunteer, I admire you. And like I said, my contribution is to help you through my workshops, peace retreats, and meditative conferences so you can live your mission profoundly and stay in the presence of the light yourself. Proud of all of you for being there as light workers for humanity. May God embrace your personal life so you can live love in your own family life as well.

Most people leave their physical body keeping a to-do list in their brain or regretting not having more time. While we live our daily life, we enter so incredibly profound in our body's shape, the intellectual problem-solving part of our brain, and our emotional reactions that we live through those 3D superficial aspects of our self, instead of seeing what we are really made of—intelligent stem cells, energy shifting so we can move our body, oneness consciousness, vital light, inner stillness, a vibration like a calm melody, just to name a few. We create a limited daily life, an after life, and a next life. We become so attached to the human realm, so caught up in it that we create a rebound system, one life after the next through the free-will to-do list.

Could we take a last walk through our life, feeling grateful for all the blessings, teachings, and so many years of union, and then detaching completely—letting go of the family, of the belongings, of our physical body, of our country, of our not-lived dreams and goals? Would you be able to take a one-way ticket up and never return to earth? Live all our goals, ideas, in this lifetime. Be successful now. Live our dream now without fears or doubts, holding nothing back. Feel satisfied in this very moment because we choose there won't be a next life. It is a win-win situation, even if we may choose to return to the physical plane after a life of fulfillment, then we will be born in prosperity and health for we have established "abundance" in our DNA through the previous life imprints of firm steps and dream realization, allowing joy, meditation, peace, harmony, and love to be part of our daily life. So do you agree with me that we don't have anything to lose by living as if tomorrow doesn't exist?

The realm where our soul resides is based upon harmony, peace, and loving vibration, only one wavelength. No ups, no downs, no challenges, no pain. Everything at reach, creation at our disposal. Only in human form do we get to experience trials, dualities, goals and hopes, and dreams. And we become addicted to it. Addicted to the need for success achieved through hardship. Wouldn't it be a challenge to know that home, belonging, and success are already ours because our light is one with creation when we're not in physical form? Just something to think about on our walks in nature.

Yoga

I went with the flow

After some tossing and turning in the night, my pillow told me to accept the offer of the hotel Dreams. Nuria Torrero, without actually having seen a class of mine, believed in me. She knew I was exactly what the guests would need. She worked as rooms division manager for the hotel Dreams in Nuevo Vallarta and asked me to offer yoga classes. I asked if it could be tai chi, and she told me it needed to be yoga, so I doubted. Nuria was very persistent and I thank her now for that.

The night before I would give my first class, I spoke to my inner self admitting that I was insecure in the practice of yoga still. The instructor course I did was fourteen years ago already. Since my nature walk - practice was my only yoga experience I had, perhaps that was not enough to be in public in a hotel with it. The duality inside of me went on for some time, because my classes in the yoga studio had been loved dearly by every student. It had been a mix of some yoga with lots of chi gong and tai chi and people loved it. Anyway, there I was, being a little skeptical about the next day's class, but I knew I would follow through with it anyway and just when I opened up and stopped objecting a little chuckle rose in me...

'Who do you think is going to give this class, he?'

Ok, so I could rest assure, the class would be channeled. Without further worrying I appeared in the class and waited patiently while saying to the guest. 'Close your eyes and find inner silence settling itself between your eyes'.. And my body started to move in forms I had never practiced before. The most wonderful yoga class came through me. I was amazed, fascinated and eternally grateful to be able to perform such magnitude of power in exercises. 'Sandra, just stay centered, I am with you, as usual.' and I bowed my head in recognizing that ever since I had learned to tune in to the divine inner space, I had never stood on my own.

We had the best imaginable place in the hotel reserved for us, the small beach at the edge of the infinity pool, at just a few steps away from the ocean. Amazing view.

A few months later I took the challenge on to be with a six month contract as Spa Manager and on top of that offering my daily yoga classes, one on one sessions and wedding ceremonies. Success, a full blossoming of my inner flower, after so many years of growing towards the light. I marveled how I was able to use all my skills to touch as many people as possible. I had a great time. But then I returned to my restorative type of life, yoga, one on one and a few weddings, 2/4 hours work a day, and the rest was 'me-time'. Expanding the light in me, in every way possible. So with the experience I had with my former yoga and tai chi classes, my time in nature, the channeling, my healing time,..I had all the pieces of a puzzle which was leading me to be able to offer the most complete class possible. A blending of yoga postures with chi gong and channeled information offered me the right kind of spiritual connection, openness of my lower back to pass the oxygen towards my legs, my lymph nodes activated all over my body, and alpha brain waves could nurture my being with calmness, while the parasympathetic nervous system was bringing saliva establishing inner peace and serenity.

Who would have thought when I took the course for aerobics instructor/nutrition counselor and we were obligated to take a large amount of hours of yoga as well, which I disliked a lot at that time, that I would end up being a yoga addict big time. I did it at first because the instructors are getting well paid for a few hours of work, which in itself is a workout, so I would win double.

What started off as calculated, became my life's joy. I am so glad I stood my ground when doubt wanted to make me quit.

Yoga the breath of life

During my youth, I had the best judo masters teaching me, and I wasn't ready to fully absorb all their wisdom and experience. Now I comprehend they were swift like the wind, light like a feather and in control of their breath. I didn't understand the essence of their teachings. I won almost every fight, but I didn't really enjoy the benefits from my martial art practice. How could I have been so blind? All those years they were my ticket to a healthy and balanced life. I had the key right in my hand. I just didn't see it, didn't have the vision open. Like many I was caught up in the physical reality on the earth.

And as you know I had migraines, toothaches, back and knee pains, hernia in my neck,

..........Xkcsvxjzkdmcvkijjjj!!!!!! All those years of suffering. Why the heck couldn't I see the true potential those masters showed me existed in me? You can not see past that we don't 'know'.

The sequence again.. First we feel curiosity, then our mind has to trust, then our heart has to feel safe, then we practice it over and over before we can accept and apply the teaching as our truth.

Now I know and this time I don't have physical masters in front of me, I have my body talking to me, my Higher Self and I'm ready to know more. Occidental yoga starts adjusting finally a little. For a long time yoga on this side of the world was known to be 'complex postures' that only 1% of the people could practice. It was limited to gymnastics, dancers,.. Very flexible people.

When I practiced judo in Belgium, the masters coming from Japan and China used to give us 'endless' breathing classes, showing us ways to anticipate, feel the movement before it is coming. I was young and impulsive, my focus was not upon 'silence or consciousness', I was anxious and eager to win competitions. I couldn't see beyond that then. How many times did I say already 'If I would have known back then what I know now.......'

When you practice yoga, out of experience I can give you an advice: don't compare yourself with the instructor or any other student. When you feel you can do more, ego will enter your moment and you'll lose the real essence and purpose of the class. When you feel you can do less, deception will enter. You'll create the feeling in you to abandon the training. Work with your own potential, stretch to your own maximum. Close your eyes often, so you can listen to your body. Practicing yoga is a process. It takes time for your body to reshape itself. After 6 months, your belly and hips will be firmer, your heart will have a stronger and slowly beat, you will be more serene in your decisions, your shoulders stronger. When you go judging your every move, you don't stand a chance to allow this process to occur.

Your instructor, after 6 months will also have an evolution, we expand in every class, each time more flexible, more determent, deeper and profounder in the spiritual, wiser, more at ease. To us, giving a class is a privilege, a luxury. Being paid for something we truly love to do. Something we truly believe in. Something that's an investment for our future.

The general public takes our ability to move for granted. It takes several energy systems to raise our arm up, many more to find balance in a tree pose. It is so intricate and perfect that the only thing left for us to do is be grateful.

Why do I close my eyes when I give my class? I often say, when I close my eyes, nobody sees me. Serious now. For those who haven't been in my yoga classes I give on the beach: we stand in circle each person occupying the space of a petal of the lotus flower. During the entire class, I close my eyes, explaining in detail the essence in every movement. While I feel the intensity in the movements, I can connect better to the wisdom and essence of it. I can transcend the physical and explain to you how I feel, and how it benefits me. I suppose I am helping my lymphatic system to do its job by focussing upon it.

And I'm not judging you. I already know you got up early in the morning to join my class, to feel safe, it takes a large amount of self respect and responsibility to do this. Some of you leave your husband in bed to get to the class, being on your holiday or even anniversary. I see it daily, and admire you for it. So trust me, the least I'm worried about is the how much you stretch in a posture. Your intention is what counts for me. Self love flows. Want to know the secret? When you're doing a posture, feel where your limit lies, accept this has been your reality until that moment, breathe out slowly and press your stretch a little more. You'll have expanded your potential, a tiny bit,.. One tiny bit every day makes a big difference after 6 months.

I have given several workshops and classes to yoga instructors from all around the world and many of this wisdom is already practiced everywhere. I feel grateful. For some time I had a dvd of my classes and two instructors placed my class in the college they were teaching on a large screen every morning before the classes started, and all the students together practiced the beach chi yoga flow. Rewarding echo's! Thank you for the honor.

Yoga as a mixture with tai chi is as profound as it gets. The slow movements connect us to our etheric body. When we let our thoughts pass like clouds, then it happens, absence of tension settles 'inner silence', and we live through our etheric body. Sometimes it lasts just a short breathtaking moment, other times it lasts the entire class, but it happens to all of us. The etheric body is the field that is like a veil around our body, where peace and harmony increase according to our predisposition to be in it. The more we penetrate in it, the more we become peaceful. Some people can be detected from 1 mile away, you can feel that somebody special is approaching, you feel a warmth, a familiar feeling. Babies do the same, they are innocent, they can just look at the sky and be silent. They see, they are in their 'wondrous field of joy and bliss'.

When our etheric 'body' expands, we have more vitality, for prana flows through it in a constant way. The more we can tune into this field, the healthier we are, the more vitality we have. The more we tune into it, the alpha state offered to our mind is like sending our brain off to a vacation. That's why people love the yoga classes and miss it when they stop going. No more daily holidays.

The energy body is formed with channels which carry this prana energy throughout our body and starts from our seventh chakra. As Deepak Chopra says, they spread like roots of a plant. Normally our energy body receives cosmic energy in deep relaxed sleep or in tetha brain wave, meditative state.

Yet when we can learn to tune in meditation in motion through the practice of Tai Chi thus can we learn to move in our daily life, accumulating vital energy and we maintain the connection and stay healthy, vital and in harmony and peace. Our only obstruction can be our thoughts, so we learn first in our class to listen to our thought pattern. When we occupy our awareness to thoughts the inflow of cosmic energy is blocked. The more Tai Chi we practice the less thoughts we'll experience.

While we enter the etheric body in Tai Chi practicing in nature, our surrounding will be perceived as more beautiful, brighter. The color

green is more intense, the ambiance gets very soft, and a warm feeling reaches us. Our voice becomes more subtle. Our hearing, more tolerant to outside influence, we learn to block noises out. When we absorb the energy through our 'openness' and stillness, it settles as energy reserve in every chakra, and stores extra in our lower belly, from where it is send throughout the day towards our lower back region, where the cells are multiplied who will be send in turn to the rest of our body. It is all circle wise, in both directions. The vital energy is lifted up through 'kundalini' force, one part to our physical, mental and emotional body, one part back to our head and into the universe, and one part through our heart towards others. This entire process is reflected in our smile and eyes. And for those who can see it, in our aura. We learn to see totality when there is no tension. Before we enter the class we can carry a large burden on our shoulders, yet as we tune into this special embracive field, that large mountain becomes suddenly a hill from which we can see the totality of our life and solutions will flow into our mind when we drive home after the class.
Namaste ....The Spirit in me greets the Spirit in you.

'What's meditating?'

'It is being totally quiet and relaxed,
separating yourself from everything around you,
setting your mind free like a bird,
and you can then see your thoughts as if they were passing clouds.'

From the movie The little Buddha

The practice of YOGA

Relationships between the
yoga movements - asanas
daily action
and our emotions

This is fascinating information I discovered by listing to my 'inner guide'

- Our lymphatic system is incredibly important for our overall wellbeing. It is the garbage bin in our body. An ongoing recycling process. This drainage system in your body is linked up to the potential that the area represents. A healthy knee reflects serene decisions. While a damaged knee represents 'decisions taken in fear, lesser quality/decisions not accepted by us'. In short this is the process: The knee attracts our attention. When we capture the message, the stretching of the yoga movement opens the lymph boxes in the backside of the knee, and purify, cleansing the damaged old cells, then new cells generate a new opportunity. Every 'yoga stretching' pumps oxygen is the area we're working upon, so more white blood cells can be generated that maintain the immune system operating in its full potential. If we can combine 'knowledge' with yoga, then we can maintain our body, mind and emotions at vital spirit level. The question is 'how flexible' are you as to capture the messages your body sends you? How many times, did we delete documents in our computer, but forgot to empty out our trash? Without emptying, our computer stays overloaded. The same thing happens with our body. When we don't oxygen our lymph boxes enough, they can't do their duty completely; which is collecting and emptying the trash.

- Opening up our lower back. The majority of stem cells are multiplied at the height of our lower back, at the base of our spine. People call this the Kundalini rises. These new and young cells are accumulated at the base of the spine and are send to every part of our body, becoming who we will be over the next...days. Talking about 'investment'..

- Breathe with your lungs. Don't try to breathe with your chest, or with your belly. Breathe the pure air, 'life force' in with your lungs at the side of your rib cage and feel how the breath extends from your lungs towards your belly and chest. I've heard many times: 'I am 30 or 40 years old and I until today I didn't know how to breathe.' It shocks many.

Breathe the air in, and allow the oxygen to flow in your bloodstream all over your body, breathing out through every cell.

In tai chi this it's of vital importance to feel every cell and unite them as one in your mind. Feel, sense the union, like the waves of the ocean in 'yoga', unity of little drops, intelligent cells with a nucleo, a center that is in love with you whatever your thoughts are. Inner stillness is always at reach, waiting for our attention. The 17 liters of blood is pumped all around our body, while you exhale, stretch and release all tension. And when you breathe out peaceful, this peace spreads all over your entire being. Your head feels lighter, being in the alpha brain wave sequence.

-And most of all…Activate your parasympathetic nervous system by focusing on saliva in your mouth. Peace will embrace you instantly.

White Light Vinyasa
Suriana Maskar

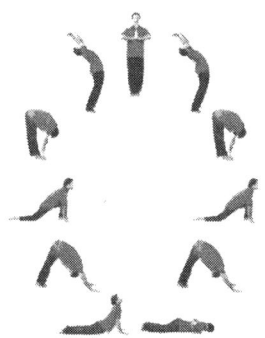

1. We embrace the sacred space, Prana, from open arms we start uniting our hands and honor the White Light, bringing our hands

towards our chest, paying attention to our thymus gland. We allow love in.

2. Raising our hands, we curve our back slightly backwards and relax our lower back the sacred space we penetrate with our hands. When we practice this in the open air, we observe where our hands finish and the eternal sky begins. Is there actually a separation? Inside a hall, see how your hands penetrate the air surrounding you and feel the prana (life force) existing in the union.

3. Opening up our elbows we bring our arms down, looking at our hands, bending our back until reaching as low as possible with our elbows towards the ground. We honor the space we occupy on earth. Greeting mother earth, we release our hands and place them on the side of your feet, stretching our lymph boxes behind our knees. Our knees have always turned toward every angle we decided to face in life, and now we allow fresh oxygen in them.

4. The left leg is being stretched out to the back and we bring both feet together.

5. Hands firmly placed on our mat, centering our body and "stand a tall mountain". Firm steps in live, being responsible, represent this tall majestic mountain.

6. Releasing all effort while we arch our back and represent a peaceful valley in our life. Allow the safe valley to be part of our NOW-moment in **full satisfaction**. It is the most difficult thing to do, accept a peaceful quiet, non-active moment when it arrives, (we tend to seek to occupy ourselves as soon as possible). Inner satisfaction is an allowance of the truth to settle.

7. Again the tall mountain. Commitment and dedication. It is our task in daily life to expanding peaceful moments until we feel content and linger even in our actions.

8. Coming back up with our left leg to the front first. Honor your space on earth and bring your arms to the chest.

Touching our thymus gland, and we start all over again, repeating several times the same sequence.

Physically we achieve more muscles in our shoulders, arms, wrists, abs and emotionally and mentally we know we can achieve peace even when we're doing an effort, through the slow breathing out with a sigh we establish inner stillness.

Inner Warrior of Light

The power of a warrior is to be reliable, trustworthy, strong and in the same time serene and loving. And serenity starts with inner satisfaction for received blessings.

Virabhadrasana 1 2 3

1. While we raise our hands we first feel every blessing we have and are in our life, today, now. Our goal, being it feeling grateful for every value, virtue, talent we have obtained until this very day. With the left foot forward we feel our current blessings recognized and accepted. With our right foot forward we feel our future blessings and heart desires to become a manifestation.

2. While our hands slight forward and stand in the warrior pose 2 we rest our hand upon the air and know that no storm can bring our lighthouse down, nor lower the density of our light.
"I aim for my goals to become manifested" representing a firm, balanced warrior, aiming to be successful in that which we pursue.
We aim for our future goals, dreams, heart desires.
Activating the law of attraction. who are you, what do you want, what are you ready to achieve in this life. Ready to embrace it as soon as it arrives in your daily life? The power of the law of attraction cannot activate when we don't recognize that which we

have already and affirm what we want to add, or don't find a silent center from which to co-create it. Knowing we are ready to take firm steps in its direction, leave the 'how' to the universe.

3. Inhaling deep. Place your foot firm and gently raise your leg to the back in unison with one arm, then both arms forward.
<u>Individual</u>: first one hand forward, then both until you feel you have reached a straight line from your hands to your leg. Variation is to bring one hand to the ground and raise the other up, shifting your hip to fit your body in. And continue with the side twists, never taking it further than your body is able to turn.

<u>Group</u>: Usually we practice this pose in a circle with several others and hold each other's hands while closing our eyes.
Like the birds that fly in a V-formation, one by one a powerful warrior of light flies up front and leads the rest. We need each other in order to keep balance and soul expansion activated.
In cycling we take this on. Each person, one by one, volunteers to pull the others forward.

Tree Pose

TREE POSE

A tree branch moves with the breeze,
bends with the storms,
and still it doesn't break.
A leaf from a tree falls in due time, in elegance and grace.

The roots, expanding in the dark wet earth, reaching for nutrition,
...on and on, faithful.

Root your foot, focusing on the center point in your foot where we connect with the magnetic field of the earth. When we raise our leg, we know the roots are solid and expanded inside the earth.
We focus on the foot that is standing solid.
Left leg, sweet side. Right side, warrior, responsible, determent side.
Then we ground ourselves. Knowing very well who we are. Confident, and intuitive, taking firm steps when needed, other times, just being still and let it all settle.
We stand tall, chest open.
When a strong wind appears, the branches won't break, for we are flexible, not rigid. Our arms can be open like branches, or against our chest, honoring the inner stillness even in challenging postures.
Our leg can be
• pulled back, opening the quadriceps
• in the normal hooked tree pose, as close as possible to your ingle.
• brought into the lotus posture, representing a lotus in a tree. One step more advanced. This advanced pose has helped me to prepare my knee to sit longer in the meditative lotus posture. Each time I stood the pose, I pushed my knee as much downwards as possible, relaxing my thighs meanwhile to activate the oxygen in my lymph nodes. Three in one.

I couldn't practice this for many years, due to my knee and lack of balance. After six months of lotus tree pose and daily effort, I proudly announce that I can stay in front of the ocean, in the sand and be a majestic tree.

Tree pose, in oneness with nature

By ourselves, choose a tree that has no ants we stand close to a tree and place one hand on the truck while standing in posture or against a tree with our back absorbing the vital force of the tree.
Standing against the tree feels so great when we can fully relax ourselves against it, closing our eyes and breathe the power of the tree in. A soothing, warm encounter. Ever tried it?
In group: I have about 5 variations according to the group and the skills. Sometimes we part with a tree in our center and make a few chains. The first person in line, absorbs the power of the tree and installs it in his/her being. The person who touches him/her needs to

focus profound on the tree, and so on, it always gets tougher to feel the tree. But the unity form is precious to see and be part of. Or we form small groups where our hand unite in the center of the circle, standing on the side, all in the same direction, and when we close our eyes, it is interesting how there is always one person at a time who holds the group up, in turn. This can be done with max 8 students a circle.

Last week in my class we were standing my united tree pose with 27 students, representing 12 different countries. In circle, placing one hand on the person next to us, creating the branches of a tree together, closing our eyes, trusting that true balance comes from within, not from our vision. I feel so honored to be part of such a sacred circle of likeminded people. Since this is a resort where I offered my classes, we had people from all around the world who don't know each other, and it feels wonderful to stand a united world tree and trust with our eyes closed that touching our neighbor is a safe thing to do.

Have you ever wondered? When our stem cells have done a perfect job, where do they go to? Do our stem cells return to the soil? Or back into the air…with the imprints of our experiences to enlighten the atmosphere, the earth, the sky,.. In our sacred circle, we lift our right hand, touching the highest branch in the tree and the leaf which has just been released from the tree falls down in an elegant and gracious way, our hand moves downward, representing the leaf. Feeling meanwhile gratefulness for the perfect system in our body. Our stem cells regenerating, multiplying each time in our body, then when 'the job is done', they leave in grace and stillness back to the soil or air, so new cells can occupy their place. A constant in love cycle. The tree doesn't feel sad because a leaf turned brown and falls, while a new one pops up the same day, somewhere else on one of the other branches.

Divine Abundance

With profound yoga practices and stretches, we balance ourselves out and enhance the light inside of us. Automatically, during our daily live, we share this light with others.

During these poses we send abundant light…

> 1. to our own self. Penetrating every single cell and atom of our being, accepting the universal abundance of Light.
> 2. to unknown people in the world. As a special contribution to the human race.
> 3. to enhance our loved ones.

The light shall be transformed in that which our body, mind and emotions need the most.

1. So first center. Open up your arms, one leg forward as wide as we are comfortable, stretch your legs and center one moment, with your eyes closed.

2. Sending abundant light to ourselves. I am a Light being….
   Breathe deep inhaling 'abundance', and turn your arms inwards, reaching forward, with our front leg just slightly bend. Bathing inside the colors of our aura field. Hold a few seconds, feeling the light of abundance offering us health and vitality in every single stem cell and atom.

3. Back to our center pose. That loving divine space where we nurture ourselves in the Light and then start reaching out to

others. How can we share that which we don't have? Only from our center, the fountain of life, can we pick energy up in order to share abundance with others. From this center posture, prepare to ask for love for people in need in the world, breathe deep and know that with pure intent you can make a difference in people's lives.

4. To people in the world, through time and space.

I am a channel of blessings to all those I focus upon....

Turn your arms inward again and lean halve way forward, raising your arms slightly and accepting that compassion is like a boomerang effect, you toss it with pure intent, and it returns 10 fold,.. Even though that is not the purpose of this exercise, the echo comes out of a consequence, not as an objective. With our hand forward we feel the pure cosmic light emanating from us towards those in need anywhere in the world.

Reach out and touch somebody's hand.

Make this world a better place. I know you.... do.

Have you ever been in need of a hug and suddenly you felt a warm embrace? There is always somebody watching over you.

5. Back to our center point. Again prepare with at least one deep warm breath to neutralize.

6. Sending love to our loved ones. "I embrace you dear one"

This time reach all the way forward, focusing upon those people we love, through time and distance we feel them right in front of us. We walk that extra mile for them, so now we also stretch a little deeper.

We finish in the center position and feel gratitude for our firm actions, our certainty we're doing the best we can. All is well. One breathe in our center, the fountain of life, can we pick energy up in order to share abundance with ourselves and others.

Ashford & Simpson, a song writer production team wrote several successful songs like "Ain't No Mountain High Enough", "You're All I Need To Get By", "Ain't Nothing Like the Real Thing", but the song which made a change in the world of many is "Reach out and touch somebody's hand", for the first time sang by Diana Ross. During her

concert performances of the song, Ross often had the whole crowd literally turn to their neighbors and "reach out and touch" their hands.
The song was sang by several artists and each time offered the same response, people held hands when they would normally hold a distance. I contribute to this flow of love with a Divine Abundance Vinyasa yoga.

Yoga makes our legs stronger

I keep on focusing on building more muscles around our knees and in our upper leg in order to avoid using our knees as first support, cause most of my students are complaining of knee damage or pain.
Those who practiced judo know that the blows a knee takes, falling on it constantly has a price attached to it. We suffer damage. The doctors told I would end up in a wheel chair, and indeed I was well on the way with cortisone injections to be able to keep on functioning in my sport. I had my bedroom upstairs and had to raise myself up, sitting on my steps one by one to get to my bedroom at night. Forgetting something from upstairs was forbidden those days, I surely helped my brain to make a list daily of my needs, things I needed to bring from upstairs to downstairs and visa versa. After a few months where I was unable to practice my favorite sport and going backwards in my health, I had a relationship with a professional cyclist.
He one day got off the roller system in the house, came to me, looked at my leg structure and told me to get on his bike on the roller system. I called him crazy, cause I didn't think that my knee would last 2 minutes. It cracked horribly. But when you're in love you do things to please the other, right. So I got on the bike, more to please him than to believe in the positive outcome. In my first turns it hurt like hell, but he told me to stay in movement for 7 minutes, that was the time our body needed to warm up. I did it, after about 3/4 days in this routine, I felt no more pain and I could feel a lot of strength in my muscles in my leg. He explained that cycling increased my muscle structure in my leg towards my knee, so in time I would not 'count upon my knee' yet have muscles to act with. And indeed, until today I keep on doing it.
Every day I sit on a bike, even if it is only to ride to the store to get some vegetables or I practice on my ecliptic machine at home a few

minutes. I stay loyal to a system I destroyed earlier on in my life. I can't restore the damage in the mechanism of my knee.

The cells of my knee can perhaps not regenerate a new knee. But I found a way to work around it, and every single movement that exists can be done by me these days. Absolutely everything. I shock my students. When they tell me that certain movements are impossible to them, I put their hand on my knee and bend it, and when they hear the orchestra that's in it they understand that most of my class is given in a way that we increase the muscle structure in our leg. In the first place I would suggest, teach your children to choose wisely the sport they dedicate themselves to, when it is an abusive sport like judo, that will a damage their joints, they will have to be aware of how important it is to stay in tune with the alternative capacity of the body functions.

Swimming, cycling, yoga and tai chi are a base for many sports. Even if, like in my case, it was practiced without really knowing why.

When somebody who loves you forces you into a certain healthy discipline, accept it. Pretty please.

Open shoulders

Five years of constant reminding myself to adjust my posture. Opening my shoulders. The being to tall made me curl-in a bit, and from the spiritual angle seen I was not releasing or detaching from the past in general. So the little curve I was developing was leading to a hernia, migraines, because of the lack of flow in that area.

I learned to accept my height, stand tall, and comprehend the people who are on my path, each time less judgmental, so the events became less personal.

Yoga and chi gong have offered me already so many benefits that I feel so incredibly grateful that I trusted my gradual flexibility and balance process without judging myself (too much).

Yoga is also a WAY of life

A philosophy that has proven itself trustworthy, applied.

A going back to **BASIC life in full appreciation and understanding**

1. Eating...became over the past decade for many a fast food event. "A plate of food is actually to nurture our organism and provide us with health and vitality.
2. Sleeping...to tune into a peaceful embracive state which restores our overall wellbeing and connects us to the delta, home coming brain wave state.
3. Work....mission fulfillment, prosperity with which we can enjoy grandly the luxuries the earth plane has to offer.
4. Sport, dancing, any movement....our body needs to release toxins, blood needs to circle.
5. Sexual activity....our pleasure areas offer us a portal, through which we can ignite our creative qualities, feel more connected to the source, feel extreme pleasures, which is like a wave lasting days in our system.

And project this out there....into the Universe. This is my personal BASIC LIFE list… having those attributes in my life, I feel truly rich and content.

I am grateful!
- ♥ I love to wake up to the sound of birds and nature surrounding me.
- ♥ I love to eat nice tasting food, which nurture my cells.
- ♥ I love to have friends who are sweet, kind, adventurous and I can laugh with.
- ♥ I love to dance salsa.
- ♥ I love to write, be inspired, feel enthusiastic about it.
- ♥ I love to offer conferences and workshops.
- ♥ I love to breathe fresh air in the morning.
- ♥ I love to be respected and recognized, seen for who I am.
- ♥ I love to watch inspiring touching movies.

- ♥ I love to have harmony with my daughter.
- ♥ I love to make love, cook together, take peaceful walks, have meaningful heartfelt conversations with a partner in perfect harmony and Light.

......And I open up to receive each one of these blessings.

I evolved...from a calculative business woman to a successful mom, writer, life-coach and instructor; in other words "a trustworthy friend". My income is the exact same, what differentiates is the fulfillment and excitement feeling I experience in 90% of my actions these days.

- I stopped taking the ideas, opinions, life styles from others for granted, analyzed my own behavior and thoughts and if they were not constructive, I stopped repeating them or allowing them from ruling my life.
- I stopped occupying my brain capacity with the judging of the actions of my neighbor or blood family member. The fact is that 75% of the people are in the first level of consciousness, which is based upon survival (not even of the fittest), and for each person it is a process. I shall no longer mimic their actions, I have my own issues, ideas and goals to focus upon.
- I dealt with anxiety and stress, one conscious action at a time, maintaining my steady breathe and attention on what I was doing, I stopped seeing time as a scary factor, not to be pulled into pressure to move into the next action.
- My habit to get from point A to B as quick and effective as possible, one part remained still, the being effective. Instead of rushing to get it done, I now take time to enjoy the totality and appreciate many details along the way.
- The next step was becoming the observer of my own being without feeling disappointed of my actions.
- I saw I was in a process where one step at the time I become more aware.
- I became very effective, we center ourselves, focusing on what really matters,
- I finally after lots of stubbornness, I apply (most of) the known knowledge to my life.

- Still expanding in knowledge and peace....

Meditation —The big M word!!

Why meditate?

Mostly because the knowing how to meditate is part of the process of personal inward growth.

Those who paint know, that when you add water to your paint, at first when you stir it, they stay separate, as though it's two layers, but then gradually they submerge into 'one'. At some point the paint is ready to be used, it feels smooth and easy to divide on the wall.

With each meditative attempt, we are closer to who we love to be, closer to the Light, expanding in Consciousness. The amount of times we sit in meditation, practice meditative yoga or chi gong, or sport in a connected way depends upon our need to grow in this aliveness process. Any form is all right. As long as we achieve stillness and an inner embrace.

Neutralize our thoughts

Remember from my book "Our Journey into Mastery", how I started to write? My treasured books were my center focus. I used to see parallel universes. their walk of life parallel to mine and write about it. I looked at patterns, behaviors, longings, created habits, my believes,.. while I was taking long walks. My objective had always been 'reaching to the top of the mountain as soon as possible. That changed to 'enjoy along the way'. Every step became of vital importance. And it was there and then where I established that 'it s safe to be one with myself'. Going within needs self-acceptance in the first place. And that is our toughest challenge.

When I was retreating on the island of St Lucia I had a little alarm clock I took with me and every hour of the day I had a positive affirmation on it.

It is safe to be me.
I can trust in love.
I am One with God.
I am a cannel of blessings to all those I touch in every way.

One of my friends was an Indian Buddhist, and he taught me 'Om mani Padme ohm', or 'Ek ong kar shiri wa he guru', but somehow the mantras I spoke in a known language reached deeper in me. They gave me more peace.

With every sunset I practiced a sun gazing ritual with the 12 names of God in Hebrew and I must admit that those powerful words vibrated all over my system. I have studied their meaning for more than two years, I torn it apart to be able to see the essence. And now when I say that mantra I feel I am so honored to be able to pronounce such divine words. I feel humbled by it.

When I needed to release my ex boyfriend I would practice these affirmations during hours. I was replacing them for my confused and 'missing' thoughts, and I used to repeat them over and over until I was free, until I could see nature again in all its beauty. It feels forced at first, but I was aware that missing someone so deeply could lead to the worst depression and even to the growth of a cyst and/or cancer.

So my effort to meditate was doubled because I choose to secure my safety, and I didn't wanted such a warm love to become a trap. All though I must admit that in the beginning, being in meditation was a mine field. My past, child hood memories, "could have been's", loneliness, dreams,...it all popped up as soon as I tried to enjoy the moment or be still. This is the reason why at first I meditated in action. Tai chi, chi gong, yoga and hiking, because sitting down made the mines explode. I abandoned every attempt after maximum two minutes due to the increase of confusion. All though.. I never gave up. I saw the Buddhist practice it. If he could do it, so would I one day just sit and be still.

Meditation process

In general with our first attempts..
1. At first 'no stress' is our motive.
2. When we start to learn to relax our body, it feels wonderful not to have to act or be responsible, just be.
3. The way our body is feeling offers a peaceful vibration in our brain.
4. We discover we are safe within ourselves and want more.

After accumulating 20 hours..
- We feel a little less worried or preoccupied in our daily life.
- We understand many events in our life, and cling less to them.
- The third eye activation has taken place in this stage of the process. We have established this feeling as our comfort zone.
- We are aware we're accumulating life force which passes fully through our being while being under the relaxing state.
- We get flashes of light appearing in front of our closed eyes.
- We learn to deal with confusion in our thoughts.
- We accept and can even feel proud of every single step we took in this life, and of all those times where getting up was an extra effort.

After at least 50 hours in total of inner stillness and self embraces
- Our consciousness has expanded by now and offer us the inner view active in our daily life, where we can aid others and find solutions to problems very quick by now.
- Our believes and goals have changed.
- Feeling healthier, more vital, more enthusiasm to get out of bed every morning.
- We start seeing the totality of our life.
- Our perception level in the physical plane is alert and active.
- We can start seeing through our etheric body, with a deep compassionate self awareness feeling.
- ..We notice that our encounters with people on the street these days are filled with life enhancing conversations.
- The more we tune in to the meditative relaxing vibrations we have become convinced that all is possible.

- ♥ We can communicate to our cells, express our momentary need of more vitality, ask permission to do something 'unhealthy' or crazy, and enjoy to the maximum that experience, without absorbing negative consequences. Like eat an entire cake or experiencing an impactful landing with a parachute on the hard ground.
- ♥ Wisdom is channeled to us, wisdom about prosperity, health, abundance, more joy and pleasure.
- ♥ Our focus has changed.
- ♥ We can tune into the higher realm through conscious inhaling, and move the energy through our body directing our exhaling breath. We know how to distinguish between our survival mode breathing capacity or the divine layer.
- ♥ We know it is through the astral part of our being we heal others, channel divine solutions for their problems and worries. It is through our intent to meditate that we made it this far, as to be a reliable friend to our friends and family,.. And most of all to ourselves.
- ♥ The world stopped being a lonely place.
- ♥ We offer our body the foods and water intake it really needs, our brain the music it relaxes with, our spirit the dancing, fun and excitement it feeds off and our soul then expresses itself through us in our professional realization.
- ♥ We do no longer want to 'change' our loved ones or work colleagues. We wish them to be loving and healthy.

Experienced mastery after 300 hours of practice advanced self love, inner stillness and channeling capacity

- ♥ We are now able to project our energy consciously across the country to our loved ones and be present with them with our etheric body.
- ♥ Being a healer, we can help, support and live unique experiences at will, while our physical body stays in the room at home, relaxing. The memory imprint will be the exact same as if 'you' would have lived it.
- ♥ We come out of all physical and mental illnesses.

- ♥ What once was survival out of pain and suffering, became now expansion of the light in us.
- ♥ Expansion of the intellect in awareness sharpness, towards the Collective Consciousness.
- ♥ We can tap into the Master Akashic Records.
- ♥ The question is now: exactly how much success do you want in which areas of your daily life?
- ♥ A smile became a natural spontaneous expression of your gratitude and love for others and satisfaction within yourself.
- ♥ We can be successful in everything we are undertaken unattached of the outcome, for we feel light in our daily life and can manifest together with the Creator that which we focus our attention upon, may it be in thought, word spoken or action undertaken.
- ♥ We believe our dreams can be manifested, with firm steps, focus and patience.

With each meditation, each and every single one, even those you thought they were just a frustrating attempt to meditate,.. we have accumulated more vital force in us. And it is like planting seeds, at first they stay hidden out of our view.

Silent meditations in a sitting posture:

A detail for when we start at first:
I would recommend you to sit against a wall, or lay down because we, as soon as the connection with the tetha brain waves/ astral body is established, our physical body may experience a spinning sensation.
We 'travel' deep within our consciousness at the speed of light in that moment and the shock of becoming aware of this, can make us fall suddenly. When we become more experienced and through chi gong enter in the meditative state, standing up, or sitting in lotus posture, our entire being is already prepared and will just find balance on its own. The sacred posture will lock itself in.

But remember, meditation radiance can be achieved through several portals, which you will see in a bit, through yoga, chi gong, hiking, praying, meditating in silence, sexual pleasure, singing, creative art,.. not only through silent lotus posture sitting. Being emerged in one self in such a way, we keep our brain from worrying, judging, complaining, comparing, doubting or anything along this line.

Being aware, being the observer, being in the moment,..for us to actually live the full capacity of light from our soul in daily life, is a never ending chapter in our life.

Our awareness skill to connect in ACTIVE or PASSIVE meditation depends on us being extrovert or introvert beings, in combination with our background and upbringing. If we have meditated all our life, just like I asked my daughter to do day after day, it automatically facilitates to 'just sit still and have no thoughts,..yet for most of us it is not so, so to stay in tuned with the astral and causal power, bathe in inner stillness, we may need pure warmhearted 'Carpe Diem' full enjoyment ACTIONS.

Awareness leads to a blissful, conservative, passionate, compassionate, enthusiastic, meditative life, and One moment linked to the next, and in each moment we have several portals awaiting us through which we can tune into the higher consciousness. Acknowledging them in their divine grace is all it takes for the magic to happen.

This is very advanced information for people who are really ready to understand the inter dimensional space, and how we tune into it, daily. Sometimes even without knowing it, we're in. Take the time I spend with Michael. The portal that was created when I was with him, became powerful through unconditional love, continuously renewed while we discovered each time a deeper love for each other and for ourselves. We experienced such gratitude feeling for our union, we would explode. This kind of love is the key to the highest level of portal, it is so certain, so valuable that it releases all earthly consciousness levels. I was in constant 'active' meditation during months, even 2 years later could I still tune in with it at will. There was a brightness around everything, I was so light in my daily life. It was not a one-time event that triggered this, it was the accumulation of cleansings, affirmations, self-preparing in me. And Michael from his part had lived among sheep, had become sensitive, had opened his heart chakra fully. When we met we were both in love with nature, with mother earth. So we could transcend its energy field. The moment the powerful portal opened was the moment when he felt on his knees and declared his love to be sacred. There was a sexual act, but it was not the sexual action which triggered the opening. It was the unmistakable feeling of immeasurable love which made us be so much in the moment that our surroundings disappeared and we both entered the inner space. We saw our own soul reflected in the other person's eyes. Both of us were being absorbed and embraced by the highest love possible, swept off our feet and taken into the realms of Creation itself.

Deep inside the healing knowledge

Some years ago I worked with a hotel guest who became a special friend. He had Parkinson's disease and had bought a condo in the hotel I was working. Despite of his challenge, he came faithful to my yoga classes daily.

He was one of the only people I gave more than one session in a short amount of time. Normally people leave after a week and I don't get to really go profound in healing. The first month I worked with him, I was disappointed by not seeing immediate results and I felt very tired, drained each time I had done a therapy with him. But then, I had him floating in the pool of the spa on a air mattress and after giving him a relaxing massage and I brought him in meditation where he relaxed but still kept the trembling in his body going. I opened myself up to finding the connection in him to 'stillness'. I thought that when he can be without shaking a few seconds he can imprint that upon his mind and cells as a reality, and build more health up from there. So I let words come through in the meditation. And suddenly...when I was holding his hand. Nothing. No movement in the hand that laid in mine. I was pleasantly shocked and fascinated. Then my brain became active. -I pulled myself out of the meditative state that I enter when bringing others under meditation. I accompany them at the same leve-l. So I analyzed the meditation and looked for the exact words that triggered the stillness in him. And I repeated a the last part of the meditation. And I found it, the words were 'You are light, you are a light body'. He stayed for about 5 minutes floating without no hand movement. I brought him into 'awake state' maintaining the alpha brain peaceful state activated. He looked at his hands and was able to stay conscious for about one more minute before trembling again. He hadn't been able to drink a cup of coffee without spilling it over him in years, and that moment was clearly gold to him,...and to me. That's when I stopped being tired after a session with him.

I suppose it is related to 'believe', when the person can see that there is 'hope' then faith enlightens the person and the heaviness of the doubt is absorbed. Mr D taught me much. He kept on coming daily to the yoga class and after the class I took him apart to practice a 10 minute tai chi or chi gong with his feet standing in the ocean.

Two times have we been able to tune into that 'zone' while standing up practicing chi gong. He had been cramped, bending in a forward position and after a few months of special exercises I made him do, he was standing firm up, able to open his shoulders and chest, head up. And he was able to smile again, the muscles in his face were also reacting again. When they left back to Canada, after 4 months in my yoga class every day, I arrived at my yoga spot on the beach platform and had to breathe profound to find balance, cause I missed him dearly. He had been waiting for me to arrive with his mat ready, and even though some nights he had hardly slept because of the pain, he had still been there, loyal to himself. I am so grateful to have met him and his wonderful wife who stands with him, maintaining balance in her joyous being while treating her husband with the due honor and respect. In the last conversation we shared he asked me if he should still take medicine. I told him that adding the right medicine to our intense work would improve his state even more. One week later his being 'settled' and it has been two years now that he is a stronger and healthier man, active in out door activities.

He is a changed man now, looking great, again!

When your partner is sick

How can a person deal with his partner carrying a disease, the best way?

Many people take a lifetime commitment serious, including the "in sickness and in health". So most of us have seen our loved ones suffer. Imagine it's a man loving his sick wife....

- First, don't take it personal when your partner insults you or attacks you. Embraces are key here. Get over it as soon as possible, be mature and see the reason. It's like a parent with a seven year old, when we can understand the child acts this way, because he doesn't know better, we can easily let go and relax himself with the situation and with our silly reactions. Being the mature responsible adult.
- Eat properly, health shakes, fish, white meat, veggies. Better even, accompany her on the cleansing system with flaxseed,.. So your own body is 'vital' preventing that you get emotionally out of balance as well. We all have some childhood or youth traumas tight to our system, so a neutralizing cleansing during a few months is always welcome.
- Keep on doing sport, to shake the tough times off.
- Take a few hours out with buddies.
- Pursue your dreams, keep on taking firm steps towards them.
- When a happy moment flows, make 3 knots in your tongue before provoking her to feel sad, digging out something she did in one of her weak moments, last week or last month.
- Be strong! The impotent feeling of causing worry and pain to our loved ones is a horrible feeling.
- On a peaceful afternoon, sit down with her in a place where you won't disturbed, and express how you feel with yourself in your personal growing process, goals, talents, doubts,.. Be her best friend and expose your hart, and then subtlety start touching your feelings related with the cyst, your reactions, ask her where you can support her more, how you can back her up.
- Don't take no effort she does for granted, each time she smiles with that cyst burning her energy up, is admirable.
- Allow yourself to be embraced, in hobbies, friends, or you partner. Every expression of love you can nurture in you, live it to the fullest.
- Be as patient and tolerant as you can possibly be.

- ♥ Be the example, somebody she can look up to. Doing something creative at home, where she can come and spend some time with you, relaxed, giving you a hand. She will feel useful.
- ♥ Which reminds me, when she proposes to help or do something for you, don't reject it, don't treat her like a sick person that can hurt herself, carrying a bucket. She wants to do you a favor for your kind patience and helping her through this. Say yes, let her do it. This will create a bond again. And increase her self worth.

Hang in there buddy, you're doing great!!!!
She'll come back. She has not abandoned you, she just abandoned herself for a while. Soon all of this will just be a memory where you grew stronger from. Trust in her and yourself. Her past will not haunt her anymore as soon as she's cleansed and balanced out. See the miracle happen

The next chapter: What people call astral 'traveling and OBE, please remember that this is done through focused attention where you allow yourself to be so light it feels you can fly. The reason most people need someone like me to enter in profound trance state the first time is because when they 'try' they're not capable of relaxing their body to the extent of 'mental detachment'. And as therapist, our input is vital for when a blockage appears, a shift needs to be made to change karma or enlighten their future.
Astral body journeying can reveal and better our future.

One of the many examples is this one:
The lady came to me with the need of a session for herself. But she was constantly bringing her husband in every single scene and sentence spoken prior to the meditation, so I decided to address to him first. His health had been very poor and he was of elder age, she feared for his life and did not wanted him to leave. We flew over the earth and looked for him, but we couldn't find him here, so we searched beyond this life and found him in wrapped in a dark cloud inside her vision. We reached out but he didn't see her, so he couldn't take her hand and get out of the darkness. She was desperate. So I relaxed her more profound and took her back to her own path where I asked her to expand in light so she would be more powerful to help her loved ones. She passed

purification, she dropped the load she was personally carrying, then she saw her future filled with opportunities in her mission where she leads others to a more fulfilled life. And about an hour in 3D time later we went back to the space where we had seen her husband inside the dark cloud. Now she was ready to reach him. I looked into his potential and we saw clearly how valuable he still was on earth, so through uniting the power within me and her profound love, we managed to release him out of the grip of the dark cloud and the light shined bright in him again. Then we returned to the vision of his body on earth and this time found him feeling stronger in health living his mission, and enjoying the peace and harmonious unity with his family.

He himself had not been physically in meditation with me, yet through love, there is no real gab. And he did have the predisposition to be more loving, healthy, and believed in what his wife told him about our session.

All well.

I had this type of experience several times already where each time we've been able to pump aliveness in somebody who had a different reality awaiting. We create a positive vision that can transcend the old one. Both options stay available. The end result or outcome is not determent yet. It is our choice, and firm steps and loving decisions have to be undertaken, all along the way. I as therapist am not taking the credit, even though I love to receive the warm 'thank you' hug! The person does it by approaching me, that's where the decision is taken. That's where the shift starts occurring. Please remember that the inter dimensional meditation sessions are a process. Whatever you've experienced in that trance like state with me is real. Cleansings, purification in different organs, nervous system, karma release, needs to happen, develop itself, from the DNA imprinted cells to the actual manifested visible manifestation, or what we call change. This may take 'time', please don't doubt this process.

Love is not a fight, but something worth fighting for.

I am still very 'virgin' on this profound topic, but I truly believe the river can create branches when we don't like the flow of it. I believe strongly that we can change our life course. When compassionate true love and mission fulfillment is set as intention, the 'positive end result' is awaiting for us. The fact we are challenged to branch is perhaps placed as our real future in front of us. It takes a lot of courage and will power to overcome duality and see through the obvious, make changes and believe in love. Against all odds.

Comprehending the messages coming through our inner encounter sessions, communication with our inner guides is all very advanced and a little challenging.

Praying would be talking to God, meditating is receiving the divine response and acting upon it.

When we learn to quiet our brain can we channel information directly from the source. Then Light beings we call 'Guides' appear to lead us through thick layer between the two dimensions. Guides don't have a physical form, yet most of the time they appear to us as a person, because it increases our confidence and credibility level. The "it's real" - feeling. According to my question or subject, a different light being appears. In channeling our inner awareness connects with a guide according to the type of message or work to be passed on. We operate on several planes, and most of us are spirit guides to other people or to our own self.

My yoga classes, temazcal or private astral journey meditation sessions are always guided by my higher self/guide who in turn is enlightened by the Collective Consciousness. Our guides stay loyal to us and are perceived by us, as long as we tune in often enough. That's why it's important to dedicate a certain amount of time to 'opening the portal of light daily. You become familiarized with the realm/ guides/ home. But we all know that to actually become a family, in word and love,. It takes a whole lot of work and dedication. If it is your goal to be spiritual, live freer, light hearted, healthy,.. Then you need to become the portal. Learn to accumulate it in you, so you don't depend upon the physical space surrounding you needing to be sacred..

Out of Body Experiences

…should actually be called 'out of brain experiences'. Our focus and awareness is penetrating a warmer, brighter, more enlightened 'space', while our body rests and enjoys the benefits.

Each time my patient/friends came out of the meditation they spoke of 'Incredible beauty, THE most wonderful colors and shapes and warmhearted look of the guides'. As soon as they came back to beta state, they found earth to be 'boring and primitive'. I myself could 'feel' and know what is happening, yet I had not yet 'seen' what they see. I started by 'acknowledging why' I wanted to have these 'out of brain' experiences: I wanted to touch my loved ones who lived at distance, be able to aid my daughter in her school; for myself personally, rejuvenate, train my body, feel sensual, swim in the depth of the ocean and build up more enthusiasm, optimism and youthful spark of life in my being. When we learn to tune in profoundly, then the experience lived in the vision inside the meditative state is accepted as real to our being, as if it really took place. The unlimited expression and possibilities of the spirit body, while we relax and observe, imprints the changes and experiences upon my cellular structure and if we can settle it, it becomes part of our DNA as a life transcending change.

Powerful channelers like Edgar Cayce have confirmed that in times of Atlantis, people were able to travel through time and space using a large crystal. -Did our species evolve actually?-

My daughter, when she's under meditation and we ask the guide to take me somewhere in time space, it happens each time by my guide touching a flat crystal from which light emanates and then we are being transported to the 'place of my request'. Even when I ask for information about an specific time or event, the guide puts his/her hand over the crystal and then the answer appears to them. I like to believe they tune in to our 'MASTER AKASHIC RECORD'. A giant library where all our future and past experiences and potential is stored.

I recommend you to open up only to 'Reach a higher consciousness level, touching soul and spirit. Then this objective intention is like your navigational tool in the mediation. After a few days, several messages will appear, write them all in your diary, even if not comprehended.

So now, how to OBE out of brain travel safe?

1. Sit or lay in a comfortable posture with the predisposition to relax and with every slow exhaling breath, feel self love entering every part of your being.
2. Repeat 3 times 'I raise my awareness to a Higher state of Consciousness. I open up to the conscious experience of floating out of my physical state, with the protection, help and support of God. I am a Light form.'
75% of your being will focus on the inner traveling, 25% will remain focused on your immediate surroundings.
3. Focus upon the center between your eyebrows, while your eyes close, and you stop having visual opinions. Let the sounds from your surroundings become exterior to you, without influencing you.
4. Feel stillness overtaking.
5. Choose to observe your thoughts, allow them to pass like the clouds, without paying any further attention to them.
6. Focus upon the center between your eyebrows and let your face muscles relax.
7. Your thoughts are each time more subtle, further away. You'll feel it when you enter the twilight zone. Your head and heart will be light and your body heavy..
8. Feel these words inwardly, very peacefully 'I am aware only of the loving consciousness of my astral body.''
9. After this stay with the words 'Light form', and imagine a guide next to you who touches a round large crystal, from which a light emanating through which you journey. Enjoy……..

Journey back

- See or perceive the light-spiral-formed portal and return to the physical plane through it. Bring your physical body back in to awareness. Let your brain take over and think of 'returning fully with my awareness back into your body'.
- Breathe deep and at ease.
- Right before you return you have the option to do a good deed and ask for abundant love and light to be bestowed upon your loved ones and upon those in need.
- Feel grateful for the experience and close the portal, giving thanks to the guide who accompanied you in the safe journey within.

- Don't move to quick. The theta brainwave heaviness pressures still upon us, activate your movement with hands, neck, feet and then open your eyes, turning to the side before raising yourself up.
- As soon as you can, write all the details from the experience down. Remember, the universe has a sense of humor, and many messages come as a metaphor.

Solution oriented or victim oriented?

- Wholeness healing
- Mental imprints
- Trauma relief
- Doubt and worry release

Our brain has many experiences accumulated. According to the life we have lived, most of us have spaces where it is better not to journey to. One thought can make us travel back to our past, and bring it back to the future.

The solution oriented general action is to learn to express our needs, our ideas, our opinions, instead of living in wishful thinking that those who surround us can guess what we want. In the process of being listened to, you, as a person will feel validated, have attention enough. AND you will no longer have the need to dive into those old traumas in order to accumulate some self-worth or be embraced. The solution to the problem lies in the same area, you see, as we know already, the throat chakra has three exits.

- To the back we have the detachment capacity, dealing with the release of destructive events or traumas.
- One to the front, being: outer expression and communication.
- In the center, inner communication capacity

When you're learning to express, detach and communicate, then you can go inward and say 'All is well with me'. Only then can you find stillness inwardly.

We all need a WHOLENESS being. To know how health and healing works; the recognition of who we truly are.

Daily life comes without a manual, doesn't it?

We're suddenly part of other people's lives, and there hasn't been a FULL being established, so we keep on filling ourselves with 'those who surround us'. At which point in our lives do we actually choose to BE who we truly ARE, without extra imprints? Not saying we can't learn for the experiences, not saying parents shouldn't educate us, just saying we never had a chance to get to know who's actually inside of us. Who speaks, who thinks, who acts? Or more advanced, what does my soul wants from this life, how can I expand in light?

Perhaps that's what being MATURE is.. a steppingstone to being WHOLE.

Wholeness being, healing & success meditation

For the next healing and success affirmations to manifest itself I suggest you record them with your own voice, gently spoken and very slowly. Take a few short pauses and play some instrumental music in the back. Correctly done it will take you at least 12 minutes recording. If you feel the need, you can still adjust some of the sentences so they have a more profound echo that resonate more with you. Just note that most of the words are keywords and should be used.

At least three times a year, prioritize during 21 days. One time each day you sit or lay down in relaxation and consciously listen to the information, devotionally breathing it into your system. Focusing on being grateful is key to activate the manifestation. —When a child is praised, he is she will automatically perform better in the future, right? Our inner system is like an innocent child, sensitive and receptive to praise, gratefulness and affection.—

During those 21 days listen to the words over and over while you are sleeping, so you can settle this powerful resource in your system and restore your potential.

I strongly suggest to enhance this meditation with a salt shower.

And if a physical healing in a particular area needs to occur, I recommend that, before entering the relaxation, to first read the matching chakra prayer in order to uplift your inner connection; become more compassionate.

I now allow my body to relax itself fully.
I have abundant saliva in my mouth, each time more and more.
My hips start relaxing, now my right leg relaxes, my left leg relaxes. The relaxation of my lower body is so much that my knees and feet feel very light.
I focus on my upper body now. My chest, my arms, my shoulders feel very relaxed, very light.
Always lighter, and lighter.
My facial expression relaxes and my lips form a grateful smile. I let my jaw ease itself fully.
It feels safe and embracive to allow myself to be fully peaceful.
All of the muscles are now fully relaxed. I can feel the strength within my body, yet know I can rest now.
Knowing I am safe, I feel each time more and more relaxed.
I no longer control my breath, I just listen to it as a gentle caress.
I am aware of the prana, life force existing all around me and this air enters my lungs.
I feel so grateful.
My blood contains the right amount of pure oxygen, benefited with life force.
My heart beats peaceful and strong.
My coronaries conduct the blood to each corner of my heart.
The arteries in my system perform each time better their task.
As the blood circles it is balancing it all out. Offering a perfect nutrition while it reaches each one of the stem cells.
In such a manner that each one of their functions is in perfect harmony with the wholeness of my body.
No matter what my daily situation will be, each one of my stem cells is being guided by the larger blueprint that seeks the absolute best for me.
The harmony is perfect in my entire being.
My brain feels free and light.
It feels incredibly easy and natural to use my thoughts for stem cell regeneration, rejuvenation and to restore my overall system's potential health and vitality.
If any part of my body should need more attention, the intelligent stem cells of my body will correct and attend to it, while the life force restores the health and vitality in those needed areas.
My heart now embraces the moments where I was unable to pay attention to it.

Meanwhile I am aware that I have abundant saliva in my mouth.

Through his perfect state of peace I sense my spirit and soul so much alive in me.

My chest area feels warm and welcoming, activating my immune system to an optimal state. The warm feeling in my chest is now connected to the deepness of the theta brainwave state between my eyes.

I can feel I am floating, this is how light I am.

I feel grateful for the profound intelligence and unconditional love in my system.

In each moment am I capable to direct positively the ideal and ideas I need in order to live the best version of myself.

All of my emotional and mental reactions are peaceful and directed by free will, in full control. Especially, my thoughts remain within the serenity realm.

I know I am a pure channel for my soul and spirit to manifest itself through me in my daily actions, words and thoughts.

Each night while I relax my body and my facial expression eases fully as well and I rejuvenate from the deepest layers to the visual layers in my skin and look younger each morning when I wake up.

My health is each time better, because I will find detachment and reconciliation in each situation and I am learning to be satisfied about my efforts, which are each time more elevated in pure intent and in synchronicity with my highest purpose.

Through this meditation I feel revitalized within my system, profoundly peaceful and know that each time more often shall I find meaning and purpose to my life; recognize the wishes and express my soul and spirit through me.

Success and affluence commences to be part of my present and future because I believe in myself, in my synchronicity with creation and in the meaningful encounters I experience in the causal, astral and physical world.

I am trustworthy and have confidence in who I am becoming.

Each night I sleep peaceful and comfortably and each morning I wake up with new vitality, motivation and inspiration.

During each day I find gratefulness and excitement for the little details and gifts life offers me.

Thanks to me being able to connect to my higher self, every aspect of myself will be enhanced with more success, health and infinite love.

I am grateful.

As it is, I am a protected channel of blessings to myself and those I touch in every way.

Stepping up...stepping out

The three stages to physical disease are:
1. Emotional disturbance, leading to a chemical reaction.
2. Lingering in self-pity and doubt, deactivating the immune system.
3. Physical, mental and emotional weakness leading to physical imbalance in that particular area, causing a sickness to settle.

Your body is a messenger and it will alert you first with a whisper, then with a shout. At which stage are we willing to listen?? Or even better "anticipate" by entering often in the theta brain wave state, keeping your 7 chakras "open", and constantly regenerate a healthy cellular structure.

Returning to being your true self, is a choice one can take anytime, anywhere. The choice to be conscious and act upon the reality AS IT IS.
Nobody can force this upon you, choose this for you. It is entirely depending upon you, and you alone.
I myself wasn't capable of doing it, but would you, pretty please consider returning to your true being, now that you're still healthy, instead of using a disease to force you to return? Being One with God is not an alternative, it truly is a privilege.
Last week in my class I had a 7 year old saying she was attending the class because quote 'I really need some more peace in my life'.
In my youth, I never considered 'peace, or harmony or love a priority. I accumulated an entire wall of medals and trophies and rewards, but I never stopped to think about 'who was the person winning all of this'.
Cancer and cysts made me go within and ACT.

Release the trauma

When I work large groups, about 25% of my people, mostly women, have a bended shoulder posture. Then I know they still carry **it**: THE trauma. In order to survive, they have learned to hide it for the rest of society, but deep down inside they know that it haunts us, that it is actually too heavy to carry around.

The person in the mirror knows our past.

Losing

a loved one
a job we loved
or an animal we cared for

...can create a wound in our heart *so large* it can cause unbearable loneliness and grief, resentment, and to some of us install raw anger; and most of this, happens deep inside of us, without really being aware of it.

Heartfelt relationships, rather it is in family or friendships make our heart blossom, and when that person "leaves", one part of us dies as well. This is one battle we all need to prepare for. Even the most caring or wisest person passes through this inevitable process.

No matter *how challenging your life circumstance is at some point in time,* keep your chakras aligned to the source.

It is the repetition of the traumatic event **in our heads**, living inwardly in that chaos which gives us depression and heavy shoulders. The trauma itself lasted a certain amount of time. It had a beginning with an intense shock and then the destructive aftershock with a bitter sadness, disappointment, disrespected, unjustly treated feeling. From that moment on it is part of who you are, we have it imprinted upon our brain; there are neurons connected towards the event.

So each time we remember the person, the place where it happened or even the date, we may trigger it. Adding to it, that painful event is brought back to the surface of our thoughts each time we are experiencing another challenging moment. The feeling of sadness brings the other sad moment back.

The trauma became a drama through repetition, grander even than it was, more dangerous and fearful. By not being able to handle or release it, it feels like a full bucket we keep on carrying and one drop added spills it over. We made it, unconsciously, into an open wound, and have the feeling that 'those who will love us' may stab a knife in it.

Did you see movies where the earth is destroyed?

They represent how we see those dark traumas in our life. and for some of us, there were several dark traumatic moments and adding them up, it becomes one village next to the other, occupying the entire earth in darkness. Like in the third movie of The Matrix where Trinity and Neo, wounded, fly upward until they can touch the light which was overwhelming, but needed to dive down again to be able to destroy the 'dark forces' for good. Using the analogy of the movie, Neo entered the center of the destructive forces and convinced the leader that Agent Smith was going to overpower them and in return for him, Neo, to eliminate Agent Smith, all he asked of the destructive machine forces, was PEACE.

The trauma multiplies because we keep on bringing it to the surface, adding importance to it, grand-ening it, and with that a new destructive area of life is created. One that pops up when we're tired, or under some work load or family disharmony pressure. It appears everywhere, in those places where you used to be safe and happy. You may pass the square, or the market place and you realize you're not smiling at no one, your head feels so heavy, you just feel like being invisible. Sadness took over, somewhere between breakfast and lunch consuming our inner enthusiastic child and like a hamster chewing on creative ideas. That old trauma, not yet released raises to the surface, saying 'Let me out of here! Set me free! Can't you see you are aging before your time through it?! Idiot!'

Recognize what I am talking about?
I invite you to meditate with me in this ritual if you want to release one or several of those traumas. Read the ritual first, if needed a few times. I am female, so the meditation came for me. When you're male, just change the words around. If you're home and have a few candles, lighten them up, close your eyes, and focus on hearing my voice repeating these words. Make sure nobody can interrupt you. Pure intent, one time is enough. Once you have embraced yourself, it is over for good.
Trust me now. Soon it'll be over.

> *Ready. Envision yourself before the event. See yourself witht hat age, see your feet and hands. Then imagine your mature self arriving at the scene and caresses your head gently, warmly and tells you that all will be well and that you will be able to instantly let go when there will be hardship in your near*

future. Hold the hands of the younger person. Make her look in your eyes. Reassure her that everything will be fine. That she has the courage and strength to get through it. She is not alone, you're with her, all the way.

You feel an overwhelming empowerment feeling where you know you will be able to detach and transcend the difficulties ahead. This new imprint replaces the past imprint.

Move a little in time, passed the traumatic scene without giving it importance. Again unite your younger version with your current self. Embrace her and the fresh wound and send lots of infinite love to it.

If right now, you feel the need to cry, shout, insult, be angry,..go ahead. Don't deny yourself the right to release this load.

Remain a while within the warmth of the embrace and comprehend that the imprint that all will be well was effective. In the moment of departure you will fully detach of the wound.

See her holding your hand stepping backwards, until your hands no longer touch each other. Still stepping back she waves at you. She is so beautiful, you feel so much love for her and you remain eye contact until the very last moment you see her disappearing, wrapped in a warm cloud of courage and peace. And the last thing you remember is her sweet comprehensive smile.

Then you open your eyes and look at your hands, caress your face with the knowing she can rest now and you are free, because 'she' IS FREE.

Doubt SHALL come to pass...

My personal experience with it is this:

During my entire youth I truly believed in love.

I remember my dad having that sweet and joyous tone of voice, but when he became sharp edged and cynic I missed him so and I missed who I was with him. And not long later I lost my own identity as well; DOUBT creeped in, replacing the true love and warmth in my heart. As I grew up, I build a strong character in my creative professional and sport realization. But it is exhausting living with the layer of doubt wrapped around your heart.

At some point I realized the procedure of "doubt" and I decided I won't, can't lose my power any longer when those who surround me don't live up to their full potential.

By now, the root is deep, the stem broad. Many have sheltered under my branches and leaves. My own identity became a certainty.

The vision has been shared and established with open shoulders, repeated daily until it has settled as a truth.

A truth known can never be unknown. At some point we return to it. I am still my inner child filled with loving visions and illusions. Only this time I am sharing it already.

Doubt is our only true enemy. Keep that door locked! While still in the make believe space, I need to keep 'those old patterned' doubting Tomas, anxious thoughts from popping up.

A self-confident person is someone who has conquered the fight with the doubting Tomas. **That Tomas is the personality we took on when we left our true self, the red line, away from God.**

How did that Tomas get inside of us?

Science has discovered that 50% of our Tomas personality is installed in us before we're born. One way is through the mom releasing chemistry from the brain into the bloodstream which entered the baby's system. Like an old fashion tape recorder, called the subconscious brain, it absorbed all the information on the tape and kept it, for later use. Then from birth till 7 years of age the other half of capacity is filled. Opinions, perceptions, patterns, some based on fears and doubts, others based on success and joy. The Tomas personality is fully established with the age of 7, yet not fully activated. That comes with the age of 14, when we're shifting from alpha brainwaves to beta. Beta makes us THINK, meaning we're less in the present moment using our senses and intuition.

The information was installed only when we were in tuned with the highest frequency brain waves.

So question how to install habits, pattern that don't serve us? Tuning into the same brain waves which caused the pre program action to activate. I have done my best to 'mature' through my conscious choices, the truth is that I am getting so much better in my natural reactions. But not to the extend where I feel safe and blissful with myself. So now being a single mother not wanting to take things personal, how can I shift my awareness, so I do not harm my daughter or my own life?

Life always has options, they're either presented to you or you create them (or maybe they're always there and we just notice them thinking that we create them).

We all leave at some point. The question is, when do we see there is an option?? And how long does it take us to establish the opposite of the created doubt?
Self-confidence, is obtained through experience.
Experience offers wisdom. Wisdom is higher than intellectual calculated intelligence.

Andy, climbing out of a black hole

I'll share this true story with you…

It started with a representative of the Belgian Sport's Bond who approached me in a cycling competition asking me if I would honor him with participating in the Belgian Miss Body Building or Miss Fitness competition. I had never been interested in the amount of muscles I had because I felt it lessened my female-hood. But I was curious about the Miss Fitness championship. So the next week I registered and continued my normal daily cyclist training. In my town the word got out that I would participate in the competition and Andy, who was personal trainer approached me, asking if he could train me, for free, as a challenge. I agreed, without wanting to lift no weights, just extra abs exercises. We chose a song of Janet Jackson, because to show muscles the beat in the song is funky and a nice guide to move upon. We worked together on the flowing postures, and this would be my first stage performance in public. I was pretty nervous, but still obtained second place, from all the participating girls in Belgium, not bad at all.

The girl who won had been on special diet for 2 years and worked out hard for this championship. I ate a chocolate donut right before my performance and she almost chocked in the water she was drinking seeing me eat 'that prohibited thing'. She couldn't believe that I made second without hardly no preparation, other than living the life of an athlete. We had a great time that entire day. When they offered me my trophy, I asked Andy on the stage, but he rejected being in the spotlight.

And out of our training program companionship grew a friendship. Bowling, the movies, pool,.. weekly we went somewhere in our town together and even though he was a very silent person, we had lots of fun. I asked him once why he was such a peaceful person and he told me it was because he played the piano at home daily for several hours. His mom was bipolar and could not receive visitors at home, so I never heard him play in the two years we were close friends. One night after bowling we decided to have dinner in a restaurant and Andy fell asleep in the car while I was driving. When I arrived I saw that place was closed and decided to drive to the next town to a restaurant I knew had great seafood. But when I pulled up on the drive way, the sound of the stones under the wheels woke him up and suddenly he turned pale, white as the snow outside and started to scream and hold his head, shaking like crazy. I really didn't know what to do and stepped out of the car in a shock myself trough his reaction. He was shouting 'take me back' and I got back in the car and drove confused towards our town. Slowly he turned back into the Andy I knew and when we reached my place I invited him in and he explained, embarrassed, ashamed, but open to sharing his secret with me, and with you now as well. When he was 17, he had taken drugs during a few months, wanting to escape his 'home situation' and the drugs damaged his brain in such a way that he was not capable of going beyond his known world without loosing control. The roads he had taken before his brain damage, were the only ones accepted by his system. He never took any drugs again, yet had to live with the consequences of that tough moment in time. He loved his mother dearly and learned to distant her confused world from his' by playing the piano. From then on we stayed on safe grounds and no other event happened (that I am aware off).

When I decided to move to Spain, one of the reasons it was tough on me was Andy. It is hard to find such special friends in life and I would miss him. When we had our 'goodbye' party, I asked him if it was possible for him to transcend his fears so I could organize my party in the restaurant where he had his fit. My reason was that it was the closest restaurant where they had a piano and the food was absolutely delicious. And he agreed, spending 3 weeks approaching the place bit by bit in his car until he could park on the drive way and breathe the air in without feeling lost within. Twelve close friends of mine joined me on a round table and the restaurant was filled with people. When our party was almost over, I got up and asked in general if someone could play the piano, and Andy got up with a sigh and walked over to the piano in silence. When his hands touched the notes, every person in the restaurant turned still. All eyes were on him. I knew this was his first time playing outside of his home. And in public. About 80 people were captivated by his art performance, and I was so indescribably proud of my best friend,.. An outstanding performance, which he finished saying "for my dear friend Sandra! He looked me in the eyes and spoke, "I shall miss you every day of this life"

The restaurant owner came to offer him to play on weekends and I encouraged him to accept the proposal.

He accepted, and he made with that decision 'an impossible dream come true'. His original reason to play the piano, the "escape route", had become, through his daily practice, a powerful portal touching the hearts of many.

Tao, the way of nature.

Tao gathers energy without using force.

Force will cause the flow to cease.

The most sacred calendar

The sacred, secret calendar of Mexica (ancient Mexico) passed on from shaman to shaman during several generations.

THE most profound calendar I've ever encountered. More than a thousand people I've studied upon it fitted in perfect with their personalities, difficulties, challenges, weaknesses, and the most import thing is that it fitted 'in the moment'. It reflected clearly what their mission and purpose could be during this life time. Each person was prepared to hear this information in that exact time and live according to it, expanding their true soul's purpose and heart's desire with it into their daily lives. It's like first you cleans a jar, empty it, than fill it with 'worthwhile values'. These values tend to be present in the person already, but stay under the surface until somebody awakens it in them. This is not a quick encounter out of curiosity, but instead please take it one step at a time and work deep and sincere. It might take you up until one year to recognize the true meanings of each angle of this calendar and fit everything in your life.

I was given the calendar in old Mexican language decided to translate and share a newer version because my sign indicates that as shaman, I shall pass the true Mexican knowledge unto other cultures. Only shamans receive this information and we normally work personally with those who are ready to hear the echo of the ancestors of this mystic country.

The COSMIC TREE

Short overview:
1. TREE OF LIFE: impulsive, sensibility, spiritual leaders, pure actions
2. WIND: vivid fantasy activated, romantic, creative, love family life
3. BRIDGE: many changes, brings hidden details into the light, difficult to settle down, very loyal
4. DRAGON: warns us of future problems, honest, organized, loving
5. COBRA: keeper of the secrets of life, a fountain of knowledge to share with others, developing talents.
6. WARRIOR: protection to those they love, new beginnings
7. DEER: balance in family life and professional realization, excellent psychologist, agile
8. PEARL: guaranteed success, affective, creative,
9. STORM: karmic cleanser, temperament changeable from reserved to stormy, noble, strong communicators with God
10. LEON: caring lovers, excellent administrators, tolerant
11. MELODY: charisma, activated inner voice, calm, prosperity, blessed
12. EARTH: healers, tolerant, good listeners
13. UNICORN: need for perfection, sensitive, joyous, leading position in society
14. JAGUAR: brilliant intelligence, powerful, seductive, union in masculine and feminine energy
15. EAGLE: need to fly high in order not to be influenced by low leveled situations, easy going, loving, giving
16. OWL: strong intuition, frank and open, lasting relationships
17. SUNRISE: connection to the infinite universal mind, givers of the heart without needing in return from the other
18. SWORD: take destiny in own hands, without fear forward, noble, talented, intuitive
19. RAIN: initiate large projects, we are all one, kind, profound friendship, noble
20. LOTUS FLOWER: goodness, handling challenges in life, wonderful artistic expression capacity

How do we know our sign?

Seek in the three lists:
- days/months
- years.
- results

Example
- Date of birth: 10th of July: nr. 131
- Year: 1968: nr. 174
- Add both up: 305
- When your number is higher than 260, you do 305 – 260 = 45
- nr. 45 = COBRA is the sign.

Another example:
born April the 3th, 2001, then it is: 33+7= 40 = FLOWER

2 important details not to forget
- when you're born in the months of January or February, then you need to take one year less, when you're born on February, the 1th 1984, then you check February the 1th, year 1983.

1922	12	1935	80	1948	149	1961	217	1974	25	1987	93	2000	162
1923	117	1936	186	1949	254	1962	62	1975	130	1988	199	2001	7
1924	223	1937	31	1950	99	1963	167	1976	236	1989	44	2002	112
1925	68	1938	136	1951	204	1964	13	1977	81	1990	149	2003	217
1926	173	1939	241	1952	50	1965	118	1978	186	1991	254	2004	63
1927	18	1940	87	1953	155	1966	223	1979	31	1992	100	2005	168
1928	124	1941	192	1954	260	1967	68	1980	137	1993	205	2006	13
1929	229	1942	37	1955	105	1968	174	1981	242	1994	50	2007	118
1930	74	1943	142	1956	211	1969	19	1982	87	1995	155	2008	224
1931	179	1944	248	1957	56	1970	124	1983	192	1996	1	2009	69
1932	25	1945	93	1958	161	1971	229	1984	38	1997	106	2010	174
1933	130	1946	198	1959	6	1972	75	1985	143	1998	211	2011	19
1934	235	1947	43	1960	112	1973	180	1986	248	1999	56	2012	125

- when the sum is higher than 260, then do "number -260"

	MAR	APR	MAY	JUN	JUL	AUG	SEPT	OCT	NOV	DEC	JAN	FEB
1	0	31	61	92	122	153	184	214	245	15	46	77
2	1	32	62	93	123	154	185	215	246	16	47	78
3	2	33	63	94	124	155	186	216	247	17	48	79
4	3	34	64	95	125	156	187	217	248	18	49	80
5	4	35	65	96	126	157	188	218	249	19	50	81
6	5	36	66	97	127	158	189	219	250	20	51	82
7	6	37	67	98	128	159	190	220	251	21	52	83
8	7	38	68	99	129	160	191	221	252	22	53	84
9	8	39	69	100	130	161	192	222	253	23	54	85
10	9	40	70	101	131	162	193	223	254	24	55	86
11	10	41	71	102	132	163	194	224	255	25	56	87
12	11	42	72	103	133	164	195	225	256	26	57	88
13	12	43	73	104	134	165	196	226	257	27	58	89
14	13	44	74	105	135	166	197	227	258	28	59	90
15	14	45	75	106	136	167	198	228	259	29	60	91
16	15	46	76	107	137	168	199	229	260	30	61	92
17	16	47	77	108	138	169	200	230	1	31	62	93
18	17	48	78	109	139	170	201	231	2	32	63	94
19	18	49	79	110	140	171	202	232	3	33	64	95
20	19	50	80	111	141	172	203	233	4	34	65	96
21	20	51	81	112	142	173	204	234	5	35	66	97
22	21	52	82	113	143	174	205	235	6	36	67	98
23	22	53	83	114	144	175	206	236	7	37	68	99
24	23	54	84	115	145	176	207	237	8	38	69	100
25	24	55	85	116	146	177	208	238	9	39	70	101
26	25	56	86	117	147	178	209	239	10	40	71	102
27	26	57	87	118	148	179	210	240	11	41	72	103
28	27	58	88	119	149	180	211	241	12	42	73	104
29	28	59	89	120	150	181	212	242	13	43	74	105
30	29	60	90	121	151	182	213	243	14	44	75	
31	30		91		152	183		244		45	76	

TREE	1	21	41	61	81	101	121	141	161	181	201	221	241
BREEZE	2	22	42	62	82	102	122	142	162	182	202	222	242
BRIDGE	3	23	43	63	83	103	123	143	163	183	203	223	243
DRAGON	4	24	44	64	84	104	124	144	164	184	204	224	244
COBRA	5	25	45	65	85	105	125	145	165	185	205	225	245
WARRIOR	6	26	46	66	86	106	126	146	166	186	206	226	246
DEER	7	27	47	67	87	107	127	147	167	187	207	227	247
PEARL	8	28	48	68	88	108	128	148	168	188	208	228	248
STORM	9	29	49	69	89	109	129	149	169	189	209	229	249
LION	10	30	50	70	90	110	130	150	170	190	210	230	250
MELODY	11	31	51	71	91	111	131	151	171	191	211	231	251
EARTH	12	32	52	72	92	112	132	152	172	192	212	232	252
UNICORN	13	33	53	73	93	113	133	153	173	193	213	233	253
JAGUAR	14	34	54	74	94	114	134	154	174	194	214	234	254
EAGLE	15	35	55	75	95	115	135	155	175	195	215	235	255
OWL	16	36	56	76	96	116	136	156	176	196	216	236	256
SUNRISE	17	37	57	77	97	117	137	157	177	197	217	237	257
SWORD	18	38	58	78	98	118	138	158	178	198	218	238	258
RAIN	19	39	59	79	99	119	139	159	179	199	219	239	259
LOTUS FLOWER	20	40	60	80	100	120	140	160	180	200	220	240	260

1
COSMIC TREE

Personality and mission:
People born under this sign are accustomed to create their own territory. Each one of their actions are well-thought of and meditated upon.

They are very close to their unconscious mind and tend to be very good therapist for that reason. They are in need to channel their enormous and wonderful energy, being excellent masters or guides.

They are very quick to develop their skills and receive often revelations, even while being awake.

Their actions and ideas are pure, adjusting themselves to any situation, all though in if it were up to them, they love to be comfortable, not in difficult or challenging situations.

For the cosmic tree, there is no medium term, when they take a decision, they move forward.

This sign holds an energy that brings prosperity and success, when they learn to work with themselves and stay on the spiritual path. They are innate spiritual leaders, and don't follow no one.

Challenge:
They have to be careful, because in difficult moments they have the tendency to become depressed from a short period to the extent of becoming bipolar. Being this way, they become in need of a lot of attention and recognition.

Significance:
Where the universe starts. The cosmic tree nurtures itself from creation and expands its branches upwards into the outer space. It represents the unusual, that which breaks the rules of the established.

Sensitivity/love:
They love to spend time in their homes, are also very social with a warm character, sensible and receptive to vibrations of every sort.

They are tender, warmhearted and romantic and inwardly love stormy relationships with a lot of passion.

Powerful affirmation: If I can see it, I can realize it.

2
BREEZE

Personality and mission:
People under this sign are capable of lifting up the energy of people that are ready to listen to wise words.
They have an excellent memory and an amazing comprehensive capacity.
It's important for them to distinguish between intuition and great imaginary force they possess.
Their special gift is the possibility to pass wisdom on to others, all though they can stay lost for a long time in not finding a purpose in life, as long as they don't recognize their gift.

Challenge:
When they can't stay focused upon their goals, values and positive energy, they can become unbalanced in changing moods in one blink of an eye.
Like the wind they tend to adjust and need to be careful not to be carried away too far out of line; being very impulsive they can lose balance and become with mental or physical illnesses, by not knowing how to use wisely their intense, sometimes stormy energy.

Significance:
The breath of life. The whisper of messages through the forest, from tree to tree passed on towards those ready to hear it.
Wind is the purifier of our three essential bodies: physical, psychic and spiritual.

Sensitivity/love:
They can be very romantic and easily influenced by the moon.
They have the challenge to learn to express their feelings, express what they truly want.
Art, being creative, music, philosophy, healing others… can help to maintain them balanced.
They need to recognize that wisdom comes through a pure heart, in serenity. For them it is recommended breathing and meditation in motion (tai chi/chi gong) to balance that turmoil they often carry along with them.
Only when their partner is balanced, they are wonderful companions, loving to live a cozy family life. When they didn't choose a partner with their heart and there is no harmony, people under this sign keep on heaving the impulse to move on.

Powerful affirmation: My balance is found in my breath.

3
BRIDGE

Personality and mission:
People born under this sign, have the ability to shed creative and hopeful light over their friend's dark moments. They have the challenge to first dominate this gift upon themselves, freeing them from past pressures, pains and future doubts. They have the opportunity, once they conquer their gift, to live intensely the moment.
They can be trusted and are very good listeners.

Challenge:
They need to be careful to maintain balance in the polarities, for many of this sign enter in the chain without end of low energies, influenced by negative people, leading to times of real bad luck. Therefore it is very important for this sign to encounter the light of their soul, finding clarity in the darkness, to unblock the negative energy created on their path of life.
An opportunity for change.
When they can take as a professional realization 'help others feel the light', each in their individual way, is when they find this true balance.

Significance:
A bridge is the spiritual protection of our being. It's an opportunity to change, and represents the night in the ancient viewpoint.
It means the edges of polarities, both light/dark, day and night, but without seeing the opposites. The renovating strength of the ancient Mexicans that makes us leave routines behind, drop the anchors and discover new territories, in order to make transformations needed in our destiny.

Sensitivity/love:
They love their privacy immensely, needing their space and time to recuperate energies used while helping others with their gift.
They tend to travel and find fortune away from their birthplace, but once settled there, they love family life. Their way to live with their friends and family is realistic, respecting and based upon loyalty.
In sentimental territory, they are very passionate lovers, sometimes struggling between too much sweetness and other times inner confused energies. That's why it takes them a long time before they find their true companion in life.

Powerful affirmation: Through darkness I find the Light

4
DRAGON

Personality and mission:
People born under this sign have the ability to see ahead, anticipating for friends and family on the how to avoid to fail in life. They can see the traps where people might fall in. Yet they cannot see their own and need often a guide to lead them on their own path.
For them every challenge is an opportunity in life, building upon self-worth and values.
They are very skilled to show us our true spiritual path, which we have imprinted upon our cells.
It is important they know their past lives in order to be able to use those skills and expand their knowledge in order to help those they love in a more effective way. For it hurts them when they can't help them.
They love to organize group meetings in their community.
They need to maintain a 'good life map' where their future is outlined, to know their future has a meaning.
Doing rituals towards God, keeps them in the Light, so they don't get to deep in their mission to help others without finding the exit.

Challenge:
They tend to walk one step ahead of their friends and family, to take their future pain so they can warn them not to fall into the trap. When they do not know this blessing, it becomes a burden very heavy to carry.
They are very open to emotional influences of others. And can easily move from happiness to deep suffering in the same day.
They get very nervous, and can lose balance due to it. This is where they have the need to find a guide who brings them back on their two feet. When not they might fall in heavy depressions.

Significance:
The sacred fire is our life. Symbolizes a net for the Mayan people. Every experience is accumulated in an intricate net.

Sensitivity/love:
They are very honest, loving and very organized.
They need their partner, feeling secure with them is essential. In order to grow spiritually they should establish individual interests, not to become dependent upon their attention.

Powerful affirmation: We are that which our mind believes in.

5
COBRA

Personality:
People born under this sign possess an impressive force to confront whatever test presented in their lives.

They are magnificent counselors, because the sense of judgment and truth never abandons them. Neither the loyalty towards those who truly deserve it. They are people who use their marvelous and potent physical energy in athletics or any other discipline demanding control, dominance and corporal coordination. They love to be informed of everything and be the resourceful creative brain behind whatever group, and even if they might deny it, they love it when we recognize their job.

Challenge: during a certain period in life they become insecure of their own values. Values they start to build up through the recognition of intelligent people. They avoid direct confrontation, and they'll do anything to postpone it as long as possible.

Significance:
For the ancient Mexicans the snake was fecundation, prosperity, knowledge, who woke up the interior fire of the supreme consciousness.

According to the Mayan ancestors, the Light was transported in the spiral form of the snake, which is the creative force of the mind and the generating force of life that resides in the base of the spine (kundalini).

Sensitivity/love:
Being excellent partners, cobras are fortunate in the sentimental territory, which they need like the air to breathe. Never the less they are not easy to express their feelings, because they are with inner (unconscious) defense/fear to be hurt. Those who know them and are really important to them accept their particular way of showing their love.

They love to seduce, which they have to learn to handle with care, for when they exaggerate in it, they lose track, balance and energy.

When they are off track and use their powerful energy in the negative way they become irritated, envious. And if so they tend to start to use 'opportunism' to achieve their goals.

The moon is a powerful influence, converting them in lovers of the night, intensely sensual and sexual with their partner, where they recharge their energy to continue on their path.

Powerful affirmation. Our power rests in the wise energy which inhabits in our interior.

6
WARRIOR

Personality and mission:
Excellent seers who receive information in different ways and sources, all though they are the last ones to recognize it. They know they inherit this gift and sooner or later start using this power in order to cleanse and channel energies of old debts.

Those born under this sigh tend to overtake family businesses or restart ancient projects. They possess a strong magnetism and natural leadership, which can offer them power and fame.

Despite of being born under the sign of warrior, as soon as they become totally aware of their gift, they are protected against accidents, assaults, violence or diseases. This protection has been in their lives from the moment of birth. Never the less, they are witnesses of many bad fortunes of others.

Their mayor virtue is to help others bring into the light the hidden wise knowledge so they can understand their destiny.

Challenge
In difficult moments they need to understand they may be helping their family members to cleans out karma. Knowing they have the power to help those they love, makes the hardship less tough to live, and being conscious of this gift balances their daily life.

Significance: Death was for the Mexican people the only certainty in their life. Death is the protective energy that accompanies us when we leave our physical body. Our last caress here on earth before we depart towards our natural home.

Death is also the ultimate waking up of consciousness after thousands of small deaths along our life.

Sensitivity/love:
In this particular life, sentimentally they are very fortunate, but they have 'being faithful' as a challenge.

They tend to pay with the same coin: being sweet to those who are sweet, and hard on those who treat them that way.

In short: it is a life full with challenges, and the only way to encounter balance and Light is by being aware.

Powerful affirmation: Rebirth through clarity, profound change can be obtained through death.

7
DEER

Personality:
People born under this sign are agile, quick and adaptable. Even in other countries they adjust and create a home within themselves.
Deer are fortunate in general, many delicate leaders are born under this sign. They have the gift to pass words on in written or spoken, sustained by their analytic power. They have a triumphant mind leading them to success.
Being very just, sometimes they are abandoned by those who see that they can't take advantage of them.
They defend the cause of many, all though they battle with self-defense.

Challenge:
They are very intuitive, and excellent psychologists, all though they have to be careful not to penetrate too deep in the mind of others, for they take the risk to get lost from their own path.
When they fail to control their energy they become demanding and spoiled, humiliating others. When this happens their organism debilitates and then they might become with diseases. (never to forget this is just a temporally state, until they pay attention).
A word they cannot forget is 'balance', for the just amount of balance will make them reach far and allow them to possess all the secrets of life. Neither can they forget 'The lie lasts until the truth arrives'.

Significance: symbol of harmony, deer is the one who holds the balance between nature and humans. The beauty, agility, strength and shyness of this animal represent the soul's characters and constant evolution.

Sensitivity/love:
Comfortable life attracts them. They are very reserved with their intimate family life. They know the secrets of many but rarely show their own inner being.
They don't like to talk about their problems. And once and a while they find pleasure in entertaining others with anecdotes about the messages they learned in their daily life.
All though they have a strong character, they are very soft in their approach, and very diplomatic. While in their negative aspect, they can play a game of submission to achieve their goals.
It pleases them to be loved and accepted by many, for that puts them in a beneficial position in life.
They fall in love deeply with their partner and as soon as they have chosen their partner for life, they stay faithful. They have the tendency to be hurt at least once in their relationships.

Powerful affirmation: Showing my true nature sets me free.

8
PEARL

Personality:
People born under this sign, love harmony in every way; from the sound of music to the intellectual expressions. They are sensual beings who love quality life. Excellent food, brand clothing, exquisite perfumes, art decorations, and music above all.
Fast thinkers and their intelligence and adaptability put them in privileged places, which they don't always take advantage of.
People born under pearl are intuitive, yet are also easy to influence, which makes it a challenge to believe in themselves and daring to do the things which satisfy them personally.
Their creativity is perhaps their strongest characteristic, because they tend to be connected to the collective consciousness level into which they have easy access. They are aware the information they need is inside of them already. And just like a seed, all it takes is a place to develop it in them. That's why lakes, the ocean, woods, rivers are their favorite places to be in order to recharge the energy needed to allow the seed to grow, and the idea or goal to be structured and manifested.
They love to create new and different things, find a way to do certain jobs easier or repair what doesn't serve anymore.
The mayor virtue of pearl is that when they can connect to their inner self, they have a guaranteed success and positive outcome in every decision they take then.

Challenge:.
They can't take suffering.
Loneliness embraces them often, even in company of others, until they understand that true love will never abandon them.

Significance: Symbol of abundance and reproduction. The ancient Mexicans used this day to ask for fertility, rain for the earth in dry seasons.

Sensitivity/love:
They love family life and tranquility, because this offers them the security they need to function well in life.
They are very sociable, good partners, and even though they posses the quality to be unfaithful, they will not put a special relationship at stake, because they fear to be alone.
They live in prosperity and abundance with their family.

Powerful affirmation: I possess the seeds that make my wishes flourish

9
STORM

Personality and mission:
People born under this sign have the opportunity to comprehend how karma is formed, from the first drop, forming a cloud, turning into a storm.

They tend to pray for those who approach them because they know that in gratitude for God, the flow of positive events in our lives continues.

Affirmations work best with candles that lighten their intuition. They know that when they light a candle, they are powerful in their communication to the universe and their words are heard clearer. The petition for help is transmuted with the help of the flame, and protect their personal physical, psychic and spiritual body.

The challenge lies not no impose their truth upon others, for they are spiritual leaders and in the spiritual world there can be no dominance.

Significance: Fire in the element of water. Rain and storm. A radiant dawn after a stormy night. The rain drop as beginning of communication with the higher realms of life. This sign represents, more than any other, the payment of karma, purifying the old ways. The ancient Mexican people born under this sign tend to be priests.

Sensitivity/love:
They are noble, good and loyal people, full with light and charm, with the just sensibility to understand what people need, beyond words spoken.

Their touch is warm, sometimes 'over heating' due to their explosive tendency when pride comes up. When this occurs then they need strong people next to them, who understand that this explosion is not meant personally.

In personal relationships they have the tendency to be very reserved and colder. Their partner shall have to be someone with much self love and comprehension in order to stay united.

They can be very sensual when confidence is given to them by their partner.

They need a lot of space to realize their profession path and love many.

They are very basic in their needs and pleasant to be around.

Powerful affirmation: Everything I give is returned to me.

10
LION

Personality and mission:
People born under this sign are excellent administrators and agile strategists. Nothing escapes their control for they have developed their 5 senses and the sixth, which makes them wonderful spiritual counselors. They have a strong ability to communicate themselves and lead in communitarian work. Their ability to cut the negative energies in these communities is powerful. Nevertheless they need to become conscious of their own values first.

They need to be very careful not to try to manipulate others to lift up their ego and pride. Their innate friendliness and spiritual peace is their balance and power.

A powerful sentence could be: I am a pure channel for good.

They guide those who are insecure, make pleasurable difficult moments; associate in good causes and negotiate for them.

Challenge: As soon as they become aware of their capacity to transcend negative energies from those they love or those they encounter, they can find freedom and health. Until then they might feel sad, tired or drained not being aware of their gift that they are helping and purifying others.

Significance: The law of nature.
Justice, writings, authority and mediator between the natural and material law. The ancient builders of pyramids, observatory stations, natural sanctuaries. Guardians of traditions.
Related to ancient scriptures and symbol of great writers.

Sensitivity/love:
They are very loved and wanted, because they show their soft aspect, are romantic and protective, and very caring lovers.
They love family life and harmony at home.
After one less fortunate relationship they tend to find their soul mate with who they feel a deep bond. A challenge lies in their passionate temperament; express themselves with their partner to stay faithful.
They are tolerant with every kind of person.
They live up to what they promise and seek to have a good time in whatever situation.

Powerful affirmation: Internal peace is obtained following the course of nature.

11
MELODY

Personality:
People born as melody can tell others when to pick up the new color in their life; believe again in good fortune, return home. They are great visionaries that can predict the future. Despite of being very conservative, they promote changes to honor the ancient ways.

Their brilliant intellect takes them into finding methods to cure soul and body of their travel companions.

They can manifest art, and some even choose to take this gift professional, for they understand that manifesting their divinity, expressing in art is using the divine energies they possess. Their expression of art will be healing to others.

Being born as melody is a privilege and blessing, their past life- efforts have been rewarded. This life has the blessing of interior harmony for themselves and those that surround them.

Prosperity is theirs to hold on to.

They have the capacity to change minds and hearts and reestablish a cosmos in chaos. They love order.

They are strong defenders of ancient villages and cultures with whom they have a strong loop.

Significance: The sacred tissue between time and space. The Mayans symbolize time like a sacred thread around a wheel, where our destiny is constructed through the decisions we've been taken along our live. Our free will is powerful, but we are also guided by the wheel itself that rotates the thread. They believe 13 lives were needed in order to be born as 'melody', and 13 after that to unwind the thread. Melody is the point of return to the source.

Sensitivity/love:
In love they seek for perfection, in themselves and those surrounding them, and for too long they try to change or manipulate their partner according to their own philosophy of life. Blindly seeking for perfection, they fail to see the true beauty in themselves and in their partner, until they wake up.

As soon as they become aware of the fact that harmony is part of their daily life, they feel calm, secure, become generous and dynamic.

They maintain a great love for their Supreme Self, through the inner voice that never fails them.

Powerful affirmation: There is a time and space for every answer.

12
EARTH

Personality:
People know that life is a challenge. They have ups and downs on their path and can deal with it lightly. They don't stop until they reach their goals. Once they start walking there is no point of return.
They love to travel, discover new territories.
They have the gift of healing others ever since they are born. Healing of body and soul.
They strongly know and believe in herbal cures, intuitive.

Significance: The sacred path we walk in order to reach our destiny. A path that guides, searches, encounters and realizes. The earth symbol seeks answers and guidance looking up at that one star that attracts their attention. This symbol represents the energy in action.

Challenge:
When they are not balanced, they become irritated, exaggerating in their answers when they feel aggravated.
They have to be very careful to channel their energy on a daily bases in positive ways, for they are vulnerable to chronic illnesses, in mind and body.

Sensitivity/love:
As soon as they can open their heart to their maximum capacity, are very tolerant, comprehensive and sweet.
Very much connected to animals and later on in life also with children.
This sign is loved by many, and they need for love to flow in their relationships. They are very good in having conversations towards others, wonderful listeners, all tough they will hardly talk about themselves.

Powerful affirmation: the answers of our soul are found while we walk our path

13
UNICORN

Personality and mission:
People born under this sign learn to dominate in perfection the dark side of their being, using morality, simplicity and justice, as this is the path to harmony in daily life. Every action has prestige and strength hidden in it.

They possess a joyous character, that prepares them to continue on the journey without no return, towards the unknown territory of the Spiritual Plane. Profound passion for life automatically puts everything and everybody on the side that doesn't fit in their interests. Freud and Jung are born under this sign, their profound nature showed them the secrets to fight with the only enemy, residing within.

For the Aztec people, the ones born under unicorn are fortunate and have a disposition and exceptional capability to raise themselves spiritually in meditation.

They take on important leading positions in society to promote projects which lead to collective changes.

Their spiritual spoken word is valid as truth, when they themselves are in balance.

Challenge:
All though seeking for perfection can also become a threat sometimes, cause they become inflexible and impossible to adjust to rules and regulations of society.

They have the need to discover their true path, recognize who they like to be, for without it they walk the earth feeling lost.

Significance: Rebirth of the Ancient Villages. It symbolizes the spine, where the sacred fire climbs upon, and empowers our 7 energetic centers, who lead us to illumination. From the earth towards the Heavens. Tezcatlipoca, Spirit of the Paths of the Universe, gives us the possibility of expression of the Divine Word, emitted telepathically, through dreams or meditation. Opening up the Heavens to obtain True Love in life.

Sensitivity/love:
Being very sensitive, they sometimes live in their childhood, where they might have had deep traumas torturing them for a long time. So partners need to comprehend and cherish them with lots of love. Very trustworthy and bonded to their partner.

Powerful affirmation: The original energy is at my base and is my center.

14
JAGUAR

Mission and personality:

People born under this sign are much alike this animal; quick, strong, brave, astute and passionate. By showing courage and strength they are the example to the weaker people. They love to initiate new projects, based upon ancient knowledge. They connect to animals in a natural way and love the countryside. Are very quick in answering and thinking, with a high intelligence and intuition. They love power at all times, in every situation.

Since they have a tendency to be reserved, they tend to communicate only with those whom they trust. Jaguar loves to visit ceremonial places where they can reestablish the energy to continue on their path.

Challenge:

They need to stay balanced, constancy being their main struggle. Select their priorities wise, remain faithful in promises to themselves, live up to their word until the very end and not to raise their ego up, for then they might humiliate others, without really knowing they do. Vanity can sometimes be their challenge. This makes them forget their spiritual powers and their mission here on earth. The worst thing that can happen to them is being humiliated in public or being criticized.

Jaguars in nature hide and wait very patiently to attack from a height. When they are feeling emotionally weak they have the tendency to take advantage of the trust and press the sensitive buttons when their loved ones least expect it.

Significance: represents the strength of all animals, firmness in decision and actions. The solar system which nurtures the earth through eclipses. A dark sun, possesses and loves the earth to start new projects and cultures. Jaguars own the ancient knowledge of the Mexica culture. Of all the signs, this symbol is the one who expands the mind more to reach a high level of consciousness.

Sensitivity/love:

Being born under this sign means being very sensual, very seductive, and they love it when their partner recognizes and stimulates this in them.

They change easily in different directions, yet their home is the center focus point, and protect their family offering security at all times.

Ladies born under this sign are very seductive, possessing a magnetic attraction for both men and women.

Powerful affirmation: Total power is found in the union between the masculine and feminine energy.

15
EAGLE

Personality and mission:

The eagle has the capacity to see from above with more clarity, see the complete view on life, and not just a small part. They also dare to face the sunlight up front, realizing they are individuals and unique the way they are.

They are very ambitious and dominant, and don't like to be ordered around, nor play the followers- role in any organization.

Challenge

The eagle changes its feathers every season in order to be able to fly higher. If they suffers over it, there is a challenge of finding confidence in this 'changing wings'-process is in peace and inner silence, in order to reach the spiritual fulfillment promised with this sign. They innately know all is transitory, and the fact that their new wings will be stronger and more powerful and they don't hold on to old habits and ways of life.

In times when they don't fly high, they have the tendency to be influenced and manipulated easily and lose sight of reality, they bump into things. Flying low means being depressed.

Significance: symbol of freedom, independence and transcendent flight. Mediator between the Gods and the humans, who shows them the path to achieve the highest degree in conscience. Guiding those in need to take off the old feathers, in order to fly lighter and in resonance with his new essence.

Sensitivity/love:

Protectors of nature environments, defenders of the true needs of the animal kingdom. Being this sensitive makes them feel lonely often, for they don't always find the love offered returned to them. Only when they encounter/recognize their soul mate can they stay faithful.

Their strong point which attract many to them is their expression of joy. They have a natural grace to enjoy little things and details of life.

They tend to have friendships in every circle in the society, being very giving and caring. They have a struggle with being responsible, constantly seeking diversion, they fail often to keep a promise. When they stay in balance, they remain healthy, strong, athletic, protected by God.

They live unattached, free from the day they are born until they leave the earth, never holding crunches, never judging anyone, accepting everybody the way they are.

Powerful affirmation: The messages of God live in our heart and are expressed by our mouth.

16
OWL

Personality and mission:
Those born under this sign are great warriors, excellent intermediators to obtain peace, and privileged doctors of soul and body.
They know the road can be long, and sometimes it takes a long time to achieve something, but they always reach their goals.
They are kind, selective with words and volunteer each time they see a chance.

Significance: Two powerful birds under one sign. The owl flying in the darkness of the night, the vulture dominating the sky in the daytime. The power hidden in basic life is in the darkness, profoundly hidden inside ourselves. The link into our interior is through understanding and forgiveness.

Challenge:
They get often in the skin of others, which makes them very vulnerable to depressions and melancholia. All it takes is one decision to reestablish their own space again, and with meditation and the recognition of their mistakes, they can be free.
Through the experiences they lived, they can, adding wisdom to it, help others to stop blaming and judging themselves and others.

Sensitivity/love:
They are impenetrable beings, yet frank and open with everybody who knows how to understand others.
In those moments where their energy level is low, they tend to see their own reflection in others and blame them for their faults. It's important for the owl to understand his duality and accept himself.
In love they are sweet seducer and tend to have long and lasting relationships. The love of their life is for them 'every relationship that has passed by their life', all those who helped them, all those who thought them the art of loving in different stages of their lives.

Powerful affirmation: Through darkness I find my light

17
SUNRISE

Personality and mission:
Are intuitive and dual, like to manifest control over situations and feelings. Escape all type of frustrating situations.
They possess a high intelligence, are very prudent, courageous at the same time.
Are defender of justice. Have the tendency to follow traditional life.
Are excellent students and workers as long as it is not a tight, closed and strict schedule.

Significance: symbolizes the movement of heaven and earth.. And the internal movement of several levels of consciousness in the humane being. It is the ancient wisdom that is stored in the cosmos. In order for us to touch that wisdom we need to open up through the energy of patience and clarity. The power that transforms our mind in a subtle instrument to connect to the infinite universal mind.
The silent protecting God. The divine feminine wisdom in action.

Sensitivity/love:
They are very comprehensive with their partner. Generally have a nice character. Their word can be trusted 100%. There are true and loyal to their partner. They can be counted upon when needed. When there are changes, they know how to adjust perfectly to new situations. They will always silently protect their loved ones.
Their honest expression can sometimes come hard over to those who can't take a true opinion.
When they get out of balance they can become very irritating and individualists.
They give of the heart, without needing in return from the other, being aware that the balance will sooner or later adjust itself.
They can change their mood according to the wind. And are like flowers with thorns, handle with care, enjoy their beauty.

Powerful affirmation: All that coming from my intuition promotes positive changes in my life

18
SWORD

Personality and mission:
People born under this sign work constantly on their tests in life. They are very determent, knowing what they want they achieve it with their strong intelligence.
They know how to center their thoughts to achieve their goals, which they keep well marked and clear in the front of their mind.
They are innate leaders, very astute and sufficiently prudent to do a good diplomatic job.
They are pioneers that open new paths, without stopping to think about what they leave behind.
They have an inexhaustible energy, which cuts both ways, it might make them stressful at times. They have the best results when they live or work in natural environments.
They have a strong healing power, and some become very good surgeons.
From young age they are highly qualified with talent, intuition and imagination. They can see answers and opportunities before they have appeared. They are masters in taking advantage of opportunities in 'flight'.
Important to know is that the law of karma works instantly upon them. Yet, even though something negative happens, they know how to turn that reality around and put a lot of effort up to make it positive.

Significance: Sacred knife that cuts both sides. Used to create statues and columns. Cuts, open, penetrates. The capacity to recognize people's thoughts, reading between sentences. The one who protects the valuable warrior. It is the energy that forms the obsidian stone, black, transparent, difficult to work or shape, and for that the most appreciated among stones.

Sensitivity/love:
They have their sentiments and reason in the right balance, which provides them of unique realizations in their life.
They have a very noble heart, but it is a challenge for them to give priority to their partner. The only reason they can stay faithful in a relationship is when they can keep on working upon their professional growth and expansion.
They are very a good friend to their friends, which they have to be cautious with cause they might take pains and problems from their friend's shoulders and carry them.

Powerful affirmation: All that doesn't kill us, makes us stronger

19
RAIN

Personality:

This person has the energy flow to build upon abundance, both in the material and in the spiritual plane. He carries the symbol of friendship from the heart, and needs the other to be himself. Like water that multiplies in order to reach its goals. One individual drop next to the other.

They need to make changes, bless others, joining others in order to feel aliveness flowing through them. They join groups of people on earth to obtain changes that benefit people and planet.

They are not over ambitious, but when they have an idea, it turns into prosperity for them. They will not seek leading positions, but when they find themselves in that reality, they act very wise and humble.

They love to be around fireplaces.

They are excellent community workers.

Challenge

Their main goal in this life is to work on self- transformation. And can not forget that with their open heart they take the burdens from their loved ones as their own. And give them a chance to live their own falling and getting up, learning from their own mistakes.

Significance: Total realization through affective behavior. The strength of union. The expansive consciousness. The energy that the rain brings to have a good crop. It also means the different stages in life, seen as one. What we do for ourselves we do for others. From the individual being towards the expansion of the Universe.

Sensitivity/love:

People born under this sign are brave, noble, imaginative, spiritual guides, they can predict the future and receive messages and signals in their dreams. They have a kind character, are very giving and calm. They live for their family, being excellent father, husband, brother, son,.. Friendship is their greatest value. Their family is representing the cloud where the descended from, and if they leave their family nest, they'll always miss them very much. That's why it is so hard for most of them to find the ideal partner. They need to learn to cut the umbilical cord.

When 'rain' channel their energy negatively, can't release the cloud on time, he can get in legal problems, feel lonely, become ill easily.

Powerful affirmation: Love is found in the unity with my heart first

20
LOTUS FLOWER

Personality:
People born under this sign are leaders, they stand out. They guide and council others on their 'right path'. They transmit their knowledge. Prevent problems and extensities. They warn when a situation is insecure or unstable. They give hope to better things in the life of all those they get in touch with. They teach them to be patient and how to take advantage of opportunities.

They are strong warriors, being guided by the solar system. They show others the ancient knowledge through artistic expression.

They are eternal 'continuers' never stop, with a very clear vision on the future. Their clear perception and observation of people makes them being able to offer the best orientations possible.

They are very selective in their friendships and only open themselves to people who are extremely intelligent and profound.

Challenge
When their energy is channeled negative they can become manipulative and feed their ego which leads to less spiritual growth.

Significance:
The energy of the mission. The regenerating strength of the cycle of life. The eclipses, where sun and moon are aligned. The person who produces in abundance, clarity, related to the Flower God. A special moment, a Sunday for Christians.

Sensitivity/love:
They are romantic and dreamers, and in the same time very practical. They can conquer even the most difficult challenges. For some of them, one part of them stays in the past, living a 'could have been', feeling they haven't been able to live to the fullest yet.

They have the power to prevent disease or death that can surround their loved ones, by giving an offer to nature or send out blessings every 20 days, for the rest of their lives.

They need to protect their heart, for they have a soft touch, and are easily offended when people correct them. This defensive system can lead to heart problems in the future.

They can never forget that they are the Sun and can give light as well as burning them when they demand too much.

Powerful affirmation: Living the mission of the compassionate Son is what makes our heart beat in peace.

The application of this calendar

I had a young woman attending my classes each day of her holiday and eventually she asked me for a private session because she was feeling depressed, a chronic depression. After a wonderful massage session and powerful meditation I still found a deep loss and sadness in her, so I decided to check the calendar as last resource. I saw that her sign absolutely didn't fit the potential I saw in her, yet the day before she matched perfectly. So, for as weird as it may sound I asked her if her mom decided in the last moment to let her be born another day than her soul intended for her. She said that was not so, still I insisted she would ask her mom. A little later she came to me and told me in all excitement and astonishment that her dad had been on a business trip during her mom's labor and would have been able to arrive the next day, so the baby was held up for 24 hours.

With this in mind I placed her again under deep meditation and following the inner guidance, imprinted upon her system that she was born one day before. As you can imagine, this is a very profound sacred ceremonial meditation and should not be taken lightly.

She became more emotionally stable, more reliable in her reactions, and slowly but surely she saw she could trust her inner state. For the first time in her life she became peaceful and serene. Now she owns a yoga studio and has a wonderful family of her own.

Could there be a relation between the date of birth and the today's anxiety issues with children? Did you ever wonder why so many children have disorders? They even invented complex names and medicines for it.

Well, interesting to know is that most of the children I get to see with unstable attitudes are all born through unnecessary preprogrammed C-section.

It is shocking to know that most doctors advice healthy strong mothers to have the cesarean section, instead of natural births. "We have higher cesarean sections than are medically necessary. We do this to avoid lawsuits," explains a surgeon at Massachusetts General Hospital "If a baby is born via C-section and there's a bad outcome, you can say everything was done. But born vaginally, it could be asked why you didn't do a C-section."

If you are pregnant or have a friend who is about to give birth, I urge you to consider carefully which form of childbirth you choose. Yet please know that when childbirth is complex and a natural birth is not possible then this tends to be fitting in the soul-physical body plan and the baby will be born on the soul's chosen date.

If you need to go through C-section and the date of birth from your baby is to be determent by availability in the hospital, then feel with one hand on your heart, the other hand on your swollen belly if the date the doctors offer you is right.

Then there was a couple that came into counseling before the divorce. She worked too many hours according to her husband.

Her sign is 'rain', and rain as you'll see is the expression of many little raindrops in unity. She does community work, helping foundations to start up. She's tried so many times to stop volunteering, but it suffocated her. When we went over the calendar together, he understood she cannot change, not if he loves her for who she is. She needs it as the air itself.

They found a mutually beneficial arrangement. Two weekend of the month for the family and the other two for volunteer work. And in order to be closer to her, he decided to join her in the community work. One year later, they are happier as ever sharing her gift together.

So basically

- Affirm to have abundant saliva in your mouth, so your parasympathetic nervous system can activate itself and offer you a serene and peaceful feeling.
- Breathing out a warm embrace and a grateful feeling from our lungs into our bloodstream and stem cells.
- During the Namaste greeting, when you start and finish your yoga class, or practice the suryana maskar, place in reverence your hands upon your thymus gland. Since this gland has the gift of being in love, and aids you with a healthy immune system.
- Make sure to drink enough water and imprint the whatever abundance blessing upon it, you wish your system to absorb.
- Stretch and feel your lymphatic system do its work for you.
- When you start a meal, close your eyes 10 sec and affirm you do a healthy digestion of this food, as well as of all emotional and mental movement within your system.
- When you walk the street feel empowered, each step grounded, firmly placed on the ground you walk, shoulders open and arms relaxed.
- Remember that strong backside represent a powerful personality…work it
- A subtle smile and salute to unknown people has a wonderful echo inside your heart.
- Make choices with your hand upon your heart, open a book that guides and empowers you with your left hand.
- Dance, laugh each time you see the opportunity in front of you.
- Open your gifts and enjoy them, don't store them in your closet.
- Whatever our chakra gifted number is, live your mission in it in order to remain with affluence and in your potential.
- Repeat as many times in a day "I am now grateful to be successful, healthy, peaceful, joyous, prosperous and blessed with lots of love".
- Eat 90% healthy stem cell foods, allow yourself 10% food-gifts that really make you smile.
- Select a mantra to interrupt destructive or negative thought. Condition your brain, don't let it have unwanted words and ideas scattered all over the place. After 5 times your brain takes whatever

thought you repeat as your idea, even if you don't agree with it, or even if it wasn't originally yours.
- ♥ Relaxing is to release all tension in your body and to feel a warm glow in the center between your eyes, an embracive feeling as your shoulders and chest just rest.
- ♥ Put your excuses in the bottom drawer. Act upon that which you believe in. For instance when you love to play volleyball and some friends invite you to play, say YES and participate.
- ♥ Learn from your own emotional reactions, don't linger in them, detach and move on, each time more mature, each time a more appreciative look to the person in the mirror.

I myself am COBRA, the fifth element on the calendar.

Eternal love to you,

Sandra

Printed in Poland
by Amazon Fulfillment
Poland Sp. z o.o., Wrocław